THE
CAMBRIDGESHIRE SYLLABUS OF
RELIGIOUS TEACHING
FOR SCHOOLS

He knoweth nothing as he ought to know, who thinks he knoweth anything without seeing its place and the manner how it relateth to God, angels and men, and to all the creatures in earth, heaven and hell, time and eternity. THOMAS TRAHERNE.

THE
CAMBRIDGESHIRE SYLLABUS OF
RELIGIOUS TEACHING
FOR SCHOOLS

CAMBRIDGE
AT THE UNIVERSITY PRESS
1951

PUBLISHED BY
THE SYNDICS OF THE CAMBRIDGE UNIVERSITY PRESS
London Office: Bentley House, N.W.I
American Branch: New York
Agents for Canada, India, and Pakistan: Macmillan

First published 1949
Re-issued 1951

Printed in Great Britain at the University Press, Cambridge
(Brooke Crutchley, University Printer)

CONTENTS

CONTENTS

PREFACE

The Cambridgeshire Syllabus of Religious Teaching for Schools was first published in 1924 as a result of the efforts of an Advisory Committee consisting of members of the Church of England, the Free Churches and of teachers in various kinds of schools and training colleges. It was expressly designed to be an *Agreed* Syllabus with the two-fold object of providing a satisfactory basis for religious teaching, and of making it easier for voluntary and county schools to be grouped for the purpose of improving the secondary education of children over the age of eleven years. A detailed revision of the Syllabus was carried out and published in 1939.

When the new Education Act made religious instruction and the use of an Agreed Syllabus an obligation in County schools, the Cambridgeshire Education Committee decided to take the opportunity of preparing a new Syllabus. The task has taken nearly two years. The aim has been to remedy such defects of the old Syllabus as experience has revealed, while retaining all that has proved of value. The new Syllabus is shorter than the old and much more space has been given to continuous exposition.

The Preface to the Syllabus of 1939 promised a Syllabus to meet the special needs of the Sixth Form of secondary schools, but the task was postponed owing to the war. The work has now been done and forms part of the new Syllabus.

The Cambridgeshire Education Committee is deeply indebted to Dr Hele, Master of Emmanuel College, who presided over the Conference, to the Rev. John Burnaby, Fellow of Trinity College, who guided the work of the Drafting Committee, and to all their colleagues, for the thought and effort they generously gave over a period of two years to the preparation of the Syllabus.

The Education Committee has decided to set up a standing Advisory Council on religious education which, amongst other

things, will be concerned with methods of teaching, the choice
of books and the provision of lectures for teachers.

A fresh edition of the Cambridge Senior Bible, arranged to
conform to the present Syllabus, will be issued as soon as possible.

———

The Eagle soars in the summit of Heaven,
The Hunter with his dogs pursues his circuit.
O perpetual revolution of configured stars,
O perpetual recurrence of determined seasons,
O world of spring and autumn, birth and dying!
The endless cycle of idea and action,
Endless invention, endless experiment,
Brings knowledge of motion, but not of stillness;
Knowledge of speech, but not of silence;
Knowledge of words, and ignorance of the Word.
All our knowledge brings us nearer to our ignorance,
All our ignorance brings us nearer to death,
But nearness to death no nearer to God.
Where is the Life we have lost in living?
Where is the wisdom we have lost in knowledge?
Where is the knowledge we have lost in information?
The cycles of Heaven in twenty centuries
Bring us farther from God and nearer to the Dust.

T. S. ELIOT
The Rock

INTRODUCTION

Parliament has decided that instruction in the Christian religion shall be a recognised and indispensable part of our public system of education. The purpose of this Introduction is to consider the significance of this decision in the light of what is happening in the world to-day.

Since the Revised Edition of the *Cambridgeshire Syllabus* was published in 1939, the Second World War has been fought. It is clearly impossible to pretend that it was fought on the issue of Christianity versus Paganism. In this twentieth century there is only one cause that can enlist, for the waging of 'total war', the whole energies of peoples, and that is a threat, real or imagined, to their *freedom*. Long ago, St Augustine saw in the 'lust of domination' the moving principle of the Earthly City and its continual wars, as mutual service is the principle of the peace of the City of God. To-day, every war must be represented by both belligerents as an 'imperialist' war, forced upon them by the enemy. Freedom, and freedom only, can be felt as worth the risk of everything else. And this is the natural outcome of the history of the Western world since the Middle Ages.

For the history of these last four centuries in the West is the history of a struggle for freedom—individual, social, and national. The Christendom of the Middle Ages was a world in pupilage, unified by its recognition of the necessity of authority, and by the acknowledgement that authority is *sacred*—that 'the powers that be are ordained of God'. This unquestioning acceptance of authority by medieval Christendom was based upon certain unquestioned assumptions as to the nature of man. It was assumed, first, that he is the creation of God and therefore naturally and essentially subject to God's rule; secondly, that his natural constitution has been impaired by a Fall, that he is a congenital invalid; and thirdly, that though there is no final escape from this sickness in his present state, his Maker and Ruler has provided a cure which, if he will accept it, will fit him for his true destiny as God's willing subject in a world to come. And it is well to note that these assumptions, though the forms under which they are expressed may vary, are not peculiar to medieval Christianity: they are the common stock of Christian faith in every age. But in the Middle Ages they were held with an emphasis which led to a realistic or pessimistic estimate of man and the world, and an idealistic or optimistic estimate of the authority to which man must be subject. Because man was radically infected with Original Sin, he could not be fit for freedom. Because this world and all the glory of it was to pass away, it was not worth worrying too much about. And because the Church was the divinely ordained authority for the necessary discipline of men in this world and their guidance to the world to come, it must stand above criticism.

The transition from this medieval state of pupilage to the modern era, in which Western man has been claiming for himself the privileges of majority, the status of an adult, was marked by the two complex processes which we call Renaissance and Reformation. The Renaissance, in revolt against the pessimistic medieval estimate of man and the world, awoke men to the realisation of natural endowments and powers still surviving in the victim of Adam's Fall, and of the entrancing wonder and interest of the natural world. The Reformation, in revolt against the optimistic medieval estimate of the Church and its divine authority, awoke men as individuals to the realisation of an authority in their own hearts and consciences which possessed the sacred quality formerly claimed and admitted in the Church. In these different ways Renaissance and Reformation alike were asserting the right of man to be free—free to deploy and exercise for their own sake the powers of thought and artistic creation which had been engrossed by the Church, free to hear and respond directly to the Word of God speaking without external mediation to the soul. The theology of the Reformers, indeed, could maintain and even exaggerate the doctrine of Original Sin; but their practice implied in fallen man the survival of a capacity and a responsibility which are the very essence of a personal freedom. The unquestioned assumption of medieval Christendom, that *men are too sinful to be free*, that they cannot without mortal danger be allowed to follow their own devices, was consciously or unconsciously abandoned; and Europe was launched on that pursuit of freedom in every sphere of life which has continued to the present day.

In every sphere this pursuit has determined the characteristic features of modern civilisation in the West. In religion it has dissolved the unity of Christendom into a multitude of sects. In politics it has accentuated the same process of dissolution by fostering the rise of nationalism, while within the nation it has undermined autocracies and made self-government the recognised ideal. In the intellectual sphere its consequences have been more complicated; but they have led, directly and indirectly, to the emergence of a new unity of thought claiming authority over the minds of men, and to a subordination of the individual to society which already threatens to become a slavery in all but name. In order to understand these paradoxical results of the pursuit of freedom we have to consider first the development of the sciences and the 'scientific attitude', and secondly the rise of industrialism to which science opened the way.

In all scientific advance the motive power has been simply the assertion of the right and the duty of thinking men to ask questions unhampered by traditional beliefs. What distinguishes scientist from philosopher is that the scientist chooses out of the universe of human experience a particular field in which the validity of answers to questions can be tested—and tested more or less conclusively: the field, that is to say, of measurable movement or change in the external world. What is above all required of the scientist is the 'single eye', a complete humility in the face of fact, a resolution not to invent his own answers to the questions which he asks of Nature, but to accept the answers which Nature herself will give if the questions are fairly put. The scientist as such asks his questions simply because he wants to know the answers. But the more he asks and the more he is answered, the more comprehensive becomes his knowledge of Nature's behaviour; and much (though by no means all) of this knowledge gives him the power to make Nature his servant, a servant that can be set to work for her master with an ever-increasing efficiency. For the true scientist, this exploitation of his knowledge is not the main object of his work. His attitude to the natural world is an attitude of receptiveness and reverence. But for the man outside the laboratory, who is untouched by the joys of discovery, the value of science lies in what it can do for him; and that is its successful application to a control of Nature which is apparently without limit. What has given science its enormous prestige in the modern world is its usefulness, its dazzling promise to make man the master of those natural forces before which he has for so long cowered in helpless submission. And this is not the end of the story. The success of science in eliciting verifiable answers to the particular kind of questions which it asks encourages even the scientist, and still more the ordinary man, to suppose that all knowledge must conform to the type of scientific ascertainment, that there is no other knowledge worth having, and finally that no beliefs about the real world which are not susceptible of scientific verification can have any claim to acceptance.

Science thus steps into the place of authority in men's minds which was once occupied by religion. And it is not surprising that religion has not been willing to see the usurpation effected without resistance. In the notorious 'conflict of religion and science' there have been grave misunderstandings and faults on both sides. There has been ground enough for the complaint of science that it has had to fight for the right of free inquiry and acceptance of the legitimate conclusions of such inquiry against bitter opposition from the representatives of religion. But now that some of the dust of conflict has settled, it can be seen that what religion is bound to resist is the pretension made by or on behalf of science to *supremacy*. For this pretension involves, in the first place, the abdication of that very dignity of man which Renaissance and Reformation alike were asserting—his spiritual freedom. *Man in the exercise of his freedom*, man in his ultimate choice between good and evil, stands beyond the reach of that understanding of the uniform processes of the natural world which is the goal of scientific research. With the world of values science by its own confession has no concern, and it can therefore have no right to man's undivided allegiance. Man is too great to accept such an authority. Too great—but also too small. For, in the second place, the undesigned but inevitable result of the triumphs of scientific discovery has been to breed in man the delusion that the world belongs to him, that he can do with it what he will. It is undeniable, as T. E. Hulme wrote just before the First World War, that 'the change which Copernicus is supposed to have brought about is the

4

exact contrary of the fact. Before Copernicus, man was not the centre of the world; after Copernicus, he was.' Not only is his science liable, as it must be, to revision: his very ideals of goodness have become his own creations which he is free to discard if and when he sees fit. To such an attitude *there is no longer anything sacred.*

When we look at the fruits of this 'emancipation from God' which have matured during the last century, we may well feel, with Robert Browning as well as T. E. Hulme, that the ideas underlying the doctrine of Original Sin are nearer to the facts than the hopeful belief in human perfectibility by which it has been so generally supplanted. If science, while claiming the credit for all advances in men's standards of living and the control of disease, disclaims responsibility for the evils of industrialism and for the terrifying leap in scale of the calamity of war, it must also disclaim its competence to provide a supreme authority for human life. It can put into men's hands powers once undreamed of: it cannot prescribe the purposes for which these powers are to be used. And that these powers have been and are being fearfully misused, is now the tritest of commonplaces. The instrument and symbol of power over the natural world, conferred upon modern man by the progress of science, is the Machine. Machines need men—or women—to work them; and the large-scale organisation of machine production demands a corresponding organisation of power over the worker. The instrument and symbol of power over men's labour is Money. Neither money nor machines are bad things in themselves. But in the modern world they have come to stand precisely for the spirit of St Augustine's Earthly City—the 'lust of domination'—which is the very substance of Original Sin. Men have not been able to pursue the fascinating lure of mastery over Nature without at the same time striving to become masters of their fellows. The cult of freedom has led to the cult of power, and the cult of power is the source of all the greater evils from which we have suffered and are suffering.

The question which divides mankind to-day is whether these evils can be abated without destroying freedom altogether. It is generally admitted that if our power over Nature is to be used so that the resources of the natural world can be shared by its inhabitants and men may live together in peace and plenty, restrictions upon freedom are inevitable. There must be some limitation of the power over other men exercised by the owner of the machine. It has often been observed that there was more than a little of the Hebrew prophet in Karl Marx: that the fierce indignation of an Amos or a Micah against the cruel domination of the rich in ancient Israel and Judah lives again in the protest of Socialism in all its forms against the freedom which is freedom to wax fat upon the misery of the poor. But Marxian Communism, as a philosophy of history, is based upon the belief that the basic fact in human life is the struggle for the means of existence, and that the strong man in possession will never yield until a stronger than he shall come upon him and overcome him and divide his spoils. The oppression of the many by the few can be ended only by the class war; and the class war is a war of extermination: it cannot be waged by the methods of political discussion which have been devised by the 'exploiters' themselves in their own interests. Government by consent must for the time being give way to government by violence. The Communist thinks even worse of human nature than Augustine or Luther: he disbelieves entirely in man's natural capacity for righteousness. But he believes that the process of history, working upon men as economic animals, moves infallibly to the elimination of unrighteousness by the extinction of the oppressors. This, at least, is the orthodox creed of Communism; and it is this creed, as dogmatic and absolute as Calvin's doctrine of predestination, that gives the Communist his substitute for religion, his conviction of being the 'chosen' instrument of the historic process which is the one 'superhuman' reality.

Opposed to Communism and its programme of revolution is Democracy—as Democracy has been understood by the English-speaking peoples: that is to say, government by the consent of the governed. The believer in Democracy assumes that it is lack of wisdom rather than lack of will that hinders the solution of the problems of government. He 'trusts the people' to accept the right solutions when these have been found, and he thinks that the best way to find them is to maintain the right of every man to speak his own mind and to criticise the views of others. It is this that determines both the importance and the character of education in a democracy. The citizen must be trained not to the abdication of private judgement, but to distinguish between reason and rhetoric and to draw conclusions without passion or prejudice. But education for citizenship cannot be a training of the mind alone: it must be a real 'discipline' of the whole man. The higher the value that is placed upon freedom and independence of thought, the more necessary it becomes to secure recognition and respect for the ideals by which a democratic society should be directed.

Freedom by itself is wholly insufficient as an ideal. It cannot be more than a condition of the good life. If we hold that true brotherhood can only be established on the foundation of freedom, we must also recognise that the freedom which neglects or violates the claims of brotherhood is no true freedom. The question is, whether the ideals of Democracy can provide their own *dynamic*; or whether it is not rather the truth that men will never, unless their very existence is threatened by war, be inspired to the willing surrender of themselves to any man-made authority—to any cause of which they cannot feel that it is both nobler and mightier than themselves.

If this is the truth, it follows that the ideals of Democracy must be based upon something greater than Democracy in order to enlist the willing and confident service of free citizens. The Christian can be a democrat because he believes that men for all their weaknesses are meant to be free and responsible beings. But he can never identify Christianity with Democracy. It is the death of true religion to be accepted merely as a bulwark of the social order. If instruction in the Christian religion is rightfully included in our educational system, that cannot be *because* we want the support of religion for the principles of Democracy: it can be only because we believe that those principles are vanity unless they are rooted and grounded in the faith and service of God.

For the ultimate issue cuts deeper than any political alternative. Both Democracy and Communism are the products of an age in which, as we have seen, Man has taken the centre of the world's stage. Explicitly or implicitly, both accept for their motive and their motto the service of humanity. Both assume the sufficiency of this motive: the horizon of both is limited by the Kingdom of Man; though, while Democracy clings to the belief that humanity can be served by the goodwill of the individual, Communism (in its orthodox form) relies upon the operation of a power which uses the individual whether he will or no. But this power is like the force of gravity—a law of nature, part of the way in which the natural world works. The fact that orthodox Communism can be regarded as an atheistic religion, while Democracy requires neither religious nor anti-religious profession from its adherents, is comparatively irrelevant. Nor is it in the last resort a question of the relative status of material and spiritual factors in the real world. The choice before us is at once simpler and more tremendous. In the mind of man there exists the idea of God. Does this idea reflect, however inadequately, the truth about the world, or is it the mirage arising from man's own cravings and discontents? Has God made man, or has man made God? The Christian religion denies that the world can either be understood or be saved unless it depends both for its existence and for its salvation upon a Reality that is eternal—that is to say upon a Power surpassing the whole content of the universe of space and time. The Christian believes that this Power is the living God whose nature and whose Name is Love, and who has so ordered the world that while men can serve Him only through the loving service of their fellows, they can in the long run serve their fellows only in His strength and for His sake.

For this reason the mainspring of Christian life and work must be faith in God. The ruling purpose of Christian education must therefore be to commend to the growing mind as well as to the heart of the child such a faith in the God and Father of Jesus Christ as will bear fruit in service. The pattern of this faith must be the faith of Jesus: Christian faith is measured by its approach to the intensity of Christ's own assurance of God. We are often told that our greatest need to-day is a renewal of faith; but if the faith meant is a faith in ourselves and in our fellow-men, that is not the kind of faith which Jesus encouraged. The faith of the New Testament is indeed a victorious confidence. But it was able to turn the world upside down just because it was not self-confidence, but the fearlessness born of an absolute trust in the One Power to whom all things are subject. Because Christ's followers know that God's Kingdom is come already 'in heaven', that from all and to all eternity the Lord reigneth, they can pray that the same Kingdom may come 'on earth', and they can devote themselves cheerfully to the doing of His will here and now. Between the calm security of the Lord's Prayer, and the dismal warnings (too common in these days) that 'nothing but...' this or that panacea can save our civilisation from collapse, there is a world of difference—the difference that is made by faith.

Religious faith is always exposed to the temptation to acquiesce in things as they are, or to let history take its course, on the ground that the Lord of history knows what He is doing and will in His own time bring the world into conformity with His purpose. But the God of Christian faith is a God who will have men to be His 'fellow-workers'. The paradox of faith was familiar to St Paul. All good is of God, yet for men to 'continue in sin that grace may abound', to leave their amendment to God, is nothing less than effectively to deny Him. It is God that 'worketh in us both to will and to do': yet for that very reason we are to 'work out our own salvation'. The man who *really* believes in God *cannot* fold his hands in passive expectancy, for he hears a call to action more urgent and compelling than any other—the call of Goodness itself to the human heart and will, the call of the Gracious Giver of all good things for the grateful response of self-devotion. To teach Christianity to our children is to inspire them with the vision of the glory of God in the face of Jesus Christ, and to send them into the world willing to follow Him who was among us as one that serveth, because they know that in such service alone is perfect freedom.

RELIGION IN THE SCHOOL

The form and content of education must always be conditioned by the view taken by the educators concerning the proper end of man. And it is neither the arts nor the sciences but religion which is able to say what this end should be. The most important element in any educational system is its religious element, for whether the system expressly includes or excludes the teaching of religion, whether it is based on a positive or negative attitude towards any particular set of religious ideas, its effect will be determined by whatever answer to the religious question is implied.

A system of education must be judged by the lives led by those who have come under its influence. By this criterion again, religious education is the most important part of all education. What a man believes determines his conduct; and, as Arnold observed: 'Conduct is three-fourths of our life.' But if an educational system is to be judged by the lives of those who have come under its influence, it can be effective only through a process of living. If Christianity is a way of life, it cannot be imparted by intellectual formulations in the way that mathematics can be; it can be learnt only from experience, not from discourse; by the experience of living the life of a Christian community. 'By love may He be gotten and holden, but by thought never' (*The Cloud of Unknowing*). If religious education is to be given in a school, it can be given only through the life and learning of that school as a whole. Intellectual formulations have their place in showing that the practices and beliefs of religion are consistent with reason. But a school cannot be a vehicle of Christian education, however much Religious Instruction occurs on its time-table, if there is bad feeling between staff and students, or if bullying goes unchecked, or if there is a selfish and self-seeking head, because the attitude to life which such a school fosters must be fundamentally un-Christian.

Religious instruction, however well adapted, is not enough. The success of the Boy Scout movement is attributable to two things— the appeal which it makes to boys because its activities are imaginatively designed to suit exactly the physical and psychological needs of that particular age, and the basing of its moral training on 'doing the good deed' rather than on 'hearing the good word'. To 'learn by doing' in the sphere of religion, a child must be encouraged to perform what Professor Nairne has finely called 'the actions of religion', in particular co-operation, unselfishness, helpfulness, kindness, affection, trust. The sphere in which the child can imbibe many of the lessons of his religious education is not the classroom where Scripture instruction takes place, but the school as a whole. The school is a community, and if Christianity is a way of life, then it is living the life of the school community which affords the best opportunities for learning something of the attitude of Christianity. 'Call the world if you please', said Keats, 'the vale of Soul-making.' The school should be a microcosm of the world, little, but nevertheless made up of real contacts with others, which affords a stage where the actions of religion can be learnt and practised. Every good headmaster knows this. What a school is able to achieve in the realm of religious education depends more upon its general 'tone' than upon the classroom ability of its Scripture teachers.

Such questions as the following, based on the standards revealed in Beatitude and Parable, should be constantly before the head-master or headmistress:

Is the school so organised as to encourage co-operation as well as proper forms of competition?

Are opportunities given whereby the stronger and cleverer may help the weaker?

Is the love of animals and birds encouraged?

What does the child do for his school?

What does the school do for the village or town, or for wider causes, such as homeless children, hospitals, or missions overseas?

Does it take pains to inspire the child with a vision of goodness, nobility and beauty?

Is the grace of courtesy (one aspect of Christian love) taught and encouraged?

Is the school emphasising 'Thou shalt' as the rule of conduct, rather than 'Thou shalt not'?

On the practical answer to such questions as these depend to an important extent the Christian atmosphere of the school and the development of Christian character in it.

School Worship

The act of worship should not be merely an opening ceremony, but a preparation for the day, the influence of which will be felt throughout the day. The teacher must strive by his own demeanour, as in the presence of God, to create a sense of worship and enable the children to feel that he is really praying the prayers which he speaks.

'There are', says Dr Fosdick, 'two fundamentally opposed ideas of prayer; one, that by begging we may change the will of God and curry favour or win gifts by coaxing; the other, that prayer is offering to God the opportunity to say to us, to give to us, and to do through us what He wills. Only the second is Christian.' Every act or word or thought which helps to align our wills with God's is prayer in the Christian sense. Prayer is essentially the opening of our souls to the divine goodness and wisdom; it is far richer than mere petition. One aspect is Adoration, the recognition of the sublimity of God and His infinite love in Christ; another is Thanksgiving, the grateful appreciation of all the good gifts of our life. A third is Confession, in which self-examination removes pride and hardness of heart, and acknowledgement is made of our human failure, measured against the standard of absolute goodness revealed in Christ.

When this idea of prayer is accepted, Intercession and Petition will be rightly understood as the effort to make our desires one with the divine purpose. Such prayer releases spiritual power to an extent which the mind of man cannot measure. Its aim is not to alter God's intention; its hope is rather to prepare the way for God to effect in the world the purposes of His wisdom and His love. Prayer at its best never says 'Thy Will be *changed*', but it says wholeheartedly 'Thy Will be *done*'. Prayer so conceived is what is meant by 'asking in Christ's name', and has, manifestly, a profound influence on man; for if it be genuine it involves the ardent desire to be, so far as in us lies, ourselves the means of answering our prayer.

The following detailed suggestions may be found helpful, since careful thought must be given to the method of assembling, to the choice of prayers, readings and hymns, and to their delivery and rendering.

(i) The entry and exit of the children should be orderly and quiet. To keep a brief silence for the recollection of the presence of God may make a helpful and reverent beginning.

If the time of assembly is used also for giving out general school notices, this should be done not before, but after, the devotional act; it is desirable that the occasion should not be used for addressing the school on matters of discipline.

(ii) Each day the single act of worship, to which the Scripture reading, prayers and hymns contribute, should be planned to constitute a unity. This planning should be done well in advance, in order that the hymns and prayers used in the common assembly may be studied beforehand if their meaning is likely to present any difficulty to the children.

(iii) Planned for a period of a week or a month, the daily worship should cover a wide field of interest and truth, so that the children may learn the rich content of religion, and the range of its application.

(iv) Not the least important duty in planning the opening service is the choice of Scripture readings. These should be arresting and complete in themselves; if not immediately intelligible they may be prefaced by a brief explanation. From eight to twelve verses is a reasonable length, though some stories and parables must run to more. A passage of extreme brevity, say two verses, will be ineffective if read by a boy or girl; in the hands of a teacher it may be the reverse, if chosen occasionally; it can sometimes be read twice through with advantage. To find passages which satisfy these conditions and are exactly appropriate to the special theme governing the day's corporate act must inevitably cause the conscientious teacher much expenditure of time and thought. He will gain help from the books mentioned on pp. 179–180, especially *The Daily Reading*. These readings should normally be taken from the Authorised Version, since it is in the highest degree desirable to make the children familiar with its surpassing beauty of diction and rhythm. The teacher should realise, however, that the Revised Version is superior in accuracy (especially in the Old Testament) and must exercise his judgement when to use it. Passages from the Psalms may be taken from the Prayer Book, where the version used is Coverdale's rendering in the Great Bible (A.D. 1539).

Readings may also be chosen from sources other than Scripture—passages from works of religious literature or devotion (e.g. Bunyan's *Pilgrim's Progress*) or memorable quotations such as may be found in various anthologies (e.g. *The Inner Light*; see Book List, p. 182).

Some children, selected with care and practised beforehand, may be entrusted with the reading of the Scripture passage; this duty should be jealously regarded as a privilege. In some schools it may even be possible to go further and actually entrust the whole act of worship on a particular day or on one day of the week to the children themselves; a form, or a senior boy or girl, may be responsible, and will of course receive guidance and advice from the teacher. Where this can be successfully done it is very effective in enabling children really to participate in the act of worship.

(v) The observance of special days and seasons with appropriate prayers, lessons and hymns is of importance as an aid to reality and variety, e.g. Beginning and End of Term, Harvest and Spring-time, festivals of the Christian Year, any national crisis or rejoicing.

(vi) The act of worship should not be so long as to cause strain or beget inattention.

(vii) Prayers should be spoken slowly and as quietly as audibility permits. As a rule they should be short and terse. The teacher should employ some prayers with which the children are familiar, and which all can join in saying, and some which by their unfamiliarity will challenge thought and attention. Special consideration should be given to the recitation of the Lord's Prayer. Often it is spoken too fast and too loud; while the frequency of its repetition dulls its meaning till with many it may become little more than a mechanical form. Efforts should be made to avoid this by careful expression and illustration of its meaning and by the teacher occasionally saying it alone with proper stresses or pauses, or speaking each petition alone with the children repeating it.

(viii) It should be explained that some expressions used in prayer (e.g. 'We *beseech* Thee to hear us'; 'O Lord, hear our prayer, *and let our cry come unto Thee*') are no indications of the remoteness of God or His unwillingness to hear, but express rather the urgency and importunity which Christ Himself emphasised in His teaching.

(ix) The language of traditional Collects and Prayers when used should be explained rather than altered. Where a phrase so archaic as 'Prevent us, O Lord' occurs, a modern equivalent, such as 'direct', or 'guide', may be substituted.

The Third Person of the Holy Trinity should normally be called 'the Holy Spirit'. But since the name 'Holy Ghost' cannot be displaced in many famous hymns and prayers, it should be frequently and carefully explained to the younger children.

(x) Hymns need to be chosen with great care, since many are bad and the wording of many others is inappropriate. Many hymn tunes, also, are unworthy and should not be used. Music has for long been important in worship; occasionally a suitable piece of music played on the piano or the gramophone may be incorporated in the act of worship.

(xi) Moments of silence should add both to the reverence and to the reality of the act of prayer; but in practice, such pauses require careful handling, and, with school children, should always be brief. They should be given, not before, but after the prayer, when the mind has received guidance and should be able to use the silence with fixed attention.

(xii) If the head teacher is able to invite other members of staff to take part in conducting the act of worship, it will greatly enhance the effect of the act of worship on the corporate life of the school.

(xiii) Consideration may also be given to the use of a class prayer at the close of the school session.

The teacher is recommended to consult the List of Books on Worship on pp. 179–182.

ON THE USE OF THE SYLLABUS

The compilers wish to make plain that the object of the syllabus is to serve as a guide and not as a hard and fast scheme of actual lessons. The passages and notes grouped under each course are primarily intended for the use of the teacher who, it is hoped, will study the *Syllabus* as a whole, and, in using any section of it, freely adapt the material or add to it in accordance with his own ideas and the needs of his pupils. A school should not feel bound to adhere strictly to the age groups suggested for the courses; but, if alteration is made, care would naturally be taken to secure continuity.

THE SCHOOL NURSERY

CHILDREN UNDER 5

Nursery Schools and Nursery Classes have now won their place in the national system of education. One of the significant features of the Education Act 1944 is the importance attached to their provision. It is the privilege of the Nursery teacher to lay the foundation for the child's school life. Nowhere is this more important than in the sphere of religious education. If in the little society of the Nursery there is unselfishness and co-operation, consideration for others and respect for their possessions, if sharing is encouraged without loss of independence, if trust and affection are given and received, a child cannot fail to be influenced by this environment. In religion, as in other aspects of education at this age, the basic need is the beginning of happy and integrated personal relationships. The child is beginning his lifelong personal relationship with God, as revealed in Jesus Christ. This sense of meeting is created by what he learns to say to God in prayers and hymns, and by the personal thought of God which is gradually built up in his imagination through the pictures he sees and the first Bible stories which he hears. A child's spiritual education depends more upon this and upon the atmosphere created by the teacher than upon the conscious imparting of ideas. In addition, children of three and four have a sensitiveness and an intensity of feeling which do not occur again until adolescence. It is therefore vital in this stage, not only that the Christian pattern of behaviour should be unconsciously assimilated from living the life of the community, but also that a feeling of reverence and worship should be awakened.

To create an atmosphere of worship, then, is of great importance. This is most naturally and effectively associated with the Morning Ring, which is held in most Nursery Schools and Classes some time during the early part of the school day, although some teachers prefer to have little gatherings of even less formality. The child's religious education at this stage, apart from the influence of living a community life based upon the Christian way of living, to which reference has already been made, will mainly be associated with these simple actions and the experience they provide of friendly companionship and happy security as well as the expression of feelings of wonder and reverence.

The manner of conducting a Morning Ring will vary with every teacher and depends very much on her taste and personality. Some teachers like to have a vase of flowers, a picture or some other beautiful object as a centre of interest, around which the children gather in a semicircle or in the form of a horseshoe. When all are seated, the teacher should wait for silence; perhaps the ticking of a clock or the singing of a bird will emphasise the quietness and make an effective introduction; alternatively an appropriate piece of music may be played. The course of the little service, under the guidance of a wise teacher, will be determined as much by the children's questioning and chatter as by the teacher's planning. It can begin by the singing of a morning hymn or greeting; some child may gleefully report the arrival of a baby brother, or the children may spontaneously begin to discuss the picture in the centre; little ceremonies can be held to celebrate the children's birthdays, little festivals arranged to fit the seasons and the Christian year; many occasions will provide an interest of the moment which will form a natural focus for feeling and activity. The younger children will not at first be able to take part, but gradually their interest will be won and they will soon be eager to try to sing the hymns and repeat the simple prayers, although the teacher's talk may be framed chiefly for the older ones. Children like routine; it is therefore better to keep more or less to the same form of service; the children's own interest and spontaneity should preclude any danger of monotony. Teachers will find that the interest aroused often recurs during the day, is expressed by children in their play, and can be woven into the day's programme. Some schools like to end the school day with a short evening prayer or hymn.

Although a set syllabus of instruction cannot be followed, by the time they reach the age of five, children should be familiar with the idea of God as a loving Father who cares for us and for all living creatures; they should know something of the Christmas story, and be forming a picture of Jesus from the simplest stories about Him.

INFANTS

CHILDREN AGED 5-7

For children under seven, religious experience is mainly indirect, yet it is at this stage that the foundations of an attitude of worship and of a Christian way of living can be laid. The gaining of this religious experience and the laying of this foundation are going on all the time through the influences which surround the children in the everyday activities of the school. These influences are exercised through the ordering of the life of the school as a whole, giving expression to Christian standards and ideas; through the fullest possible development of each child, leading to co-operation and friendship with others; and, most important of all, through the influence of the teacher. Religious awareness is aroused by the faith, thoughts, words, manners and actions of the teacher and other adults in whom the child places trust and affection.

It cannot be too strongly emphasised that a child learns through doing—and it is as important in his religious training as in the rest of the school day that he should gain knowledge through experience. The school should therefore set, and keep to, firm standards of behaviour leading to self-responsibility in choice or action. For the same reason much time will be devoted to the practice and enjoyment of religious observances. The simple daily service of praise and thanksgiving, with its personal references and its relation to the passing seasons, will form the framework of the child's religious teaching.

The essence of worship lies in the feeling of wonder and joy in the presence of beauty to which little children are so sensitive— 'Heaven lies about us in our infancy'. Thus religious education with children under seven is a careful nurturing of this awareness, this sense of wonder and reverence towards God. It cannot always be confined to any particular time—it is the response from the child to life as he lives it from day to day. Conversely, there are often small incidents in the everyday life of children which call forth a talk in the Scripture lesson. A child sees a bird which has died of cold, a collection of clothes for destitute children is being

2-2

made, another child has been seen robbing a bird's nest, some-body's Grannie has died. Answering the child's questions and stilling his fears on such topics can be a part of true religious training. The children enjoy coming together and finding outlet for feelings of praise, thanksgiving, gladness, wonder, love and reverence through songs, and through simple prayers, sometimes spoken by the teacher, sometimes said or sung by the children; suggestions made by the children themselves can be used. Many infant teachers value the celebration of the children's birthdays because of the opportunities thus afforded of emphasising the homely and familiar aspects of religion. The child's fascination with the world may also find expression in the singing of favourite hymns or the speaking of poems: and by such means his interest in the life of nature may be quite naturally associated with the practice of religion.

The relation between God and Nature may be but dimly apprehended by a child; but it is a good thing for him to form the habit of associating his delight in the world of Nature with his thoughts of God. The Spring and Harvest Festivals do not exhaust his interest in Nature. On many occasions hymns, songs and nature-poems can form a link between nature-talks and worship. They may not all be strictly 'religious', but if they express in simple language the child's sense of the wonder of the universe, and his friendly feeling for birds and beasts, they belong as much to the religious festival as to the poetry lesson. This is perhaps one of the best ways in which a closer relation may be brought about between religion and the rest of the school-life. The subjects listed in 'The Celebration of the Christian Year' on pp. 23–25 are only suggestions for topics which link the children's every-day life with a sense of worship and gratitude. Many others will occur to every teacher.

What commoner question is there from children of this age than 'How was it made?' or 'Where did it come from?' con-cerning the objects which surround their daily life? From this natural interest in 'origins' it is easy to supply the idea of God as Creator; not as the Creator of the universe, for the universe is something outside the compass of a child's mind, but as the Creator of all the various natural objects with which a child is

familiar, as the Creator and sustainer of living things, as the loving
Father, who cares for his children and has made His world for
them. A child of this age needs security and love; this idea of God
as a loving Father is that most readily accepted, and is the foundation of all his later thoughts about God. It is a good thing if it is
a recurrent theme in the religious services, so that it gradually
becomes a background of his religious consciousness and of his
learning. The teacher can do much, without formal lessons, to
accustom children to this idea of God. She can help children to
think of Him as One who is interested in and concerned with their
joys and their sorrows, their successes and their failures, their needs
and their shortcomings, in all that they do both at home and at
school, and who can be talked to, quite simply, about these things.
Children can also be helped to be aware of the Holy Spirit, not by
the use of that term, but as 'God in us', always present to guide,
to comfort and to encourage. With such a background of religious
understanding Jesus is naturally accepted as the loving Father's
greatest gift to His children, and gradually, through the Gospel
stories, He is realised as One through whose teaching, example and
friendship they may grow in the knowledge of God.

The children should take an active part in the celebration of the
festivals of the Christian year. Not only is the child therein
'learning through doing', but opportunities are also afforded to
him for the expression of his own outgoing love and affection,
scope for which is as much one of his needs as a sense of security
and a feeling of being loved. The preparations for Christmas,
Easter and Harvest Festival provide opportunities for activities
lasting over many days; the arranging of a Nativity Crib, the
inventing and acting of a Nativity Play, the making of an Easter
Garden, and the planning and carrying out of a Harvest Festival
are more satisfying to the child than the passive hearing of stories
that may become stale through much repetition. Such stories,
however, often make a fresh appeal when they are made the basis
of projects in which the child plays his own part. The teacher
should feel free, therefore, to use the Scripture period for activities
of all kinds that can be associated with religious celebrations and
with the Bible story. It is intended that for the children of five
to seven years the main emphasis in the Scripture teaching should

be on the background of family life as Jesus knew it, so that they may begin to understand and enjoy the story of the life of Jesus in the Gospels. For this purpose the narrative method is clearly inadequate—if the Bible story is to become for the child a story of real people, he must not only hear about it, he must also become part of it by doing and acting. There must always be opportunities for the expression of the emotions aroused by the stories. This expression will not necessarily follow immediately after the story, but may come out later; in occupations chosen by children, such as painting, in opportunities which may later arise of showing helpfulness and kindness to friends and animals, or in play.

In the course that follows, apart from 'The Celebration of the Christian Year', the first section suggests different aspects of the life of New Testament times, which might form centres of interest round which many activities could be grouped—handwork, play-making, picture-making, writing. The child who in this way acquires a foundation of real knowledge will at a later stage be better able to appreciate the stories of Jesus through seeing them in their proper setting. The second section includes a number of stories told by or to Jesus that lend themselves particularly well to dramatic representation. Some may be acted, with much elaboration of detail and extempore conversation, others, because of the graphic way in which they are told in the New Testament, are better mimed. The Lost Sheep and the Lost Coin are examples of stories that need to be filled out by the teacher and the children together, who will use for this purpose the gradually increasing knowledge of Jewish life. The Good Samaritan is told with a wealth of detail by St Luke, and the children who find it difficult to act and speak according to plan will be better able to lose themselves in the drama if the teacher tells the story while they act. If twenty children can take part in these little plays, so much the better—the crowd of robbers, the friends and neighbours, are as important to the stories and give as much scope for realistic action as the priest, the innkeeper, the shepherd or the house-wife.

Note. The Bible references given throughout the whole of the section for children aged 5–7 are meant primarily for the teacher, and are not always suitable for the children. It is intended that teachers should build up lessons, a lesson or part of a lesson on the subject suggested, using the biblical reference in whatever way suits the plan of the lesson best.

THE CELEBRATION OF THE CHRISTIAN YEAR
God the Loving Father, Giver of All

September

God's gifts—from plants, trees and animals. Harvest for squirrels, dormice, birds.

Harvest

The Festival of the Harvest is a drama of praise and thanksgiving for the bounty of the earth. For children it is a very real festival because of its association with familiar things. There is here a two-fold opportunity for the teacher. The harvest celebration, whether it takes the form of a simple service with music and poetry, or is elaborated into a drama, may be a very personal matter based on the child's own harvest experiences in the cornfield, the orchard, the hopfield, the fruit stall at the market or in his own garden. His personal experience will be enriched if he builds up at the same time a picture of such a harvest as Jesus knew, of which glimpses are given in the New Testament. For this purpose the following references will be found useful:

The growing corn and the weeds (St Matthew xiii. 24–30).
Walking through the cornfields (St Mark ii. 23).
Corn growing on different soils (St Mark iv. 3–8).
Flowers and grass at harvest time (St Matthew vi. 28–30).
The wonderful mustard plant (St Mark iv. 31–32).
The miracle of growth (St Mark iv. 26–29).

Autumn

Provision against the winter; warm coats of animals; warm clothes and warm fires; winter stores of food; sleep and rest; rain and frost help to prepare the ground for next year's sowing.

Christmas

God's greatest gift, the Baby Jesus.

The birth of Jesus and the visit of the shepherds (St Luke ii. 7–20).

The Wise Men (St Matthew ii. 1–12).

The story of the birth of Jesus and of the visits of the shepherds and the wise men forms the natural starting-point for such activities as the making of a Nativity Crib or the acting of a Nativity Play. The teacher should tell the story in her own words, introducing only such phrases from the passages in St Luke and St Matthew as children can understand or enjoy. To the adult the passages seem simply written: but the child often gains wrong impressions because of words which are strange to him or used in a strange way, e.g. 'they were *sore* afraid'. Yet sometimes a line of poetry may give delight by its sound alone: 'Glory to God in the highest, and on earth, peace, goodwill towards men!' The *Song the Shepherds Heard* (one of the *Bible Books for Small People*, published by the Student Christian Movement Press, mentioned in the Book List on p. 176) tells the story in simple dignified language, and gives realistic touches that help to fill in the outline of St Luke's version.

January

God's care for children; the love of parents; the presentation in the temple (St Luke ii. 21–34). The stories of Baby Moses and the Child Samuel can be used in this connection. (See 'Stories told to Jesus by His Mother', p. 28.)

Spring

Emphasis on the renewal of life; baby birds, the buds of the trees, spring flowers. God's wonderful world.

Easter

No references are given here, for the story of the Death and Resurrection of Jesus must be told by the teacher in her own words. It is possible to do this very simply, without stressing the physical details of the Crucifixion. The story of the Cross should be presented as the story of God's love, and the story of Easter as the story of One who lives for ever to be the children's Friend.

Summer

The beautiful world; sun, moon and stars; plants, flowers and animals; growth; sunshine and showers; God's work and man's work; how to help in the beautiful world.

CHILDREN AGED 5

Daily Life as Jesus saw it

The stories of Jesus as a child growing up in his family, helping at home, going to school and attending worship, playing out of doors, follow the Christmas stories quite naturally. Although there is no systematic record in the New Testament of the childhood and home life of Jesus, it is possible to build up a picture of the day to day home and community life of His time. This can be done not only from the few stories of the early years of Jesus, but from the more numerous recorded stories of the events of His manhood, and the parables and stories which He told. He drew His illustrations from the world which His hearers knew, from the doings and scenes of everyday life around Him or from the life and work of the people among whom He grew up. But even all these references will not provide sufficient material to give a full background to the childhood of Jesus. The teacher has to become familiar with the pattern of life in Nazareth by wide reading of those books and commentaries mentioned in the Book List which build up the background picture; this is made from descriptions of the present-day life and customs of Palestine, and from the results of Biblical scholarship and archaeological research. This is necessary if the teacher is to tell simple stories woven around the childhood and boyhood of Jesus in such a way that they become real to the children. The stories should be developed through the children's talk of their own news, so giving the sense of Jesus growing up like other children through the same everyday experiences although in different surroundings. The starting-point of the lesson will always be the contrasting details and circumstances of the child's own life. Projects and models will help the children to build up a picture of the childhood of Jesus.

No attempt should be made to present religious ideas which are beyond the child's power of apprehension; it should be realised that many young children find it difficult to stretch their imagination beyond the limits of their own experience, and that the building up of the picture of a different home life from their own must be a gradual process. It is better, therefore, in the early lessons to recognise the child's limitations, knowing that he will picture the baby Jesus as very much like the baby at home, the shepherds as English shepherds of his own district, and the cattle stall and manger as part of the farm buildings which he knows. After a time the unfamiliar details of Eastern life will take shape in his imagination, and he will welcome them the more readily if he has not been forced too soon to abandon his own first conceptions.

Most of the lessons will have to be built up from material contained in such books as those mentioned in the section of the Book List on 'Biblical Background' on p. 163. The Bible references given below are only for the convenience of the teacher; by themselves they do not provide sufficient lesson material.

How Jesus' Mother looked after Him

The clothes he wore; the food he ate (St John vi. 9; St Luke xi. 11–12). How the meal was eaten; how the children went to bed at night (St Luke xi. 5–8).

The House Jesus lived in

The furniture; sweeping the house (St Luke xv. 8). The candles and lamps they used (St Matthew v. 15; xxv. 1–10). The house-top (St Matthew x. 27).

His Mother's Work

Drawing water from the well (St John iv. 6–7, 11). Buying grain in the market (St Luke vi. 38). Grinding the corn, heating the oven, making the bread (St Matthew xiii. 33). Making and mending clothes (St Mark ii. 21).

Farm Life and Animals

Ploughing; the ox-yoke (St Matthew xi. 30). The ox in the pit (St Luke xiv. 5). Sowing and reaping (St Matthew xiii. 1–32). Winnowing (St Matthew iii. 12). Barns (St Luke xii. 16–18). Fruit trees (St Luke xiii. 6–9). Vineyards (St Matthew xx. 1–9). Sheep and shepherds (St Luke ii. 8; xv. 4–6).

Wild Life

Flowers (St Matthew vi. 28–29). Birds (St Matthew vi. 26). Vultures (St Luke xvii. 37). Foxes (St Luke ix. 58). Wolves (St John x. 11–12). Snakes (St Matthew x. 16).

Travel

On foot (St Luke ii. 43–46). Asses (St Matthew xxi. 5–7). Camels and caravans (Genesis xxxvii. 25). Inns (St Luke ii. 7; x. 34–35). Robbers (St Luke x. 30).

Stories told by Jesus

The Good Samaritan (St Luke x. 25–37).
The lost sheep and the lost coin (St Luke xv. 3–10).
The man with the treasure (St Matthew xiii. 44).
The pearl of great price (St Matthew xiii. 45–46).
The Good Shepherd (St John x. 11–15).

Stories about People whom Jesus met

The widow and her mite (St Mark xii. 41–44).
The mothers and the children (St Mark x. 13–16).
The blind man (St Mark viii. 22–26).
The nobleman's son (St Mark x. 17–22).
The Woman of Samaria (St John iv. 5–19, 25–30, 39–42).

The Boyhood of Jesus

The journey to Jerusalem (St Luke ii. 41–42).
Jesus in the temple (St Luke ii. 43–51).
The carpenter's shop (St Matthew xiii. 55).
Fishing on the lake
The fishermen (St Mark i. 16 and 19).
Breaking nets (St Luke v. 1–11; cf. St John xxi. 1–11).
Hauling the net (St Matthew xiii. 47–48).
Daily life
Tolls (St Mark ii. 14).
Measuring grain (St Luke vi. 38).
Children's outdoor games (St Luke vii. 32).

The soldier, the tax-gatherer, and the common people
(St Luke iii. 10–14).
The blind (St Matthew xv. 14).
The Good Samaritan (St Luke x. 30–35).
The king's clothes (St Matthew vi. 29; xi. 8).
The merchant and the pearls (St Matthew xiii. 45–46).
Hiring labourers (St Matthew xx. 1–15).
The hard-working labourer (St Luke xvii. 7–9).

Religious Training
The temple (St Luke ii. 41–51).
The synagogue (St Luke iv. 16).
The habit of prayer (St Luke xviii. 1; St Matthew vi.
8–15).

Stories told to Jesus by His Mother
Stories of Joseph (Genesis xlv; xlvi. 1–7; xlvii. 1–6).
The Baby Moses (Exodus ii. 1–10).
The Boy Samuel (I Samuel iii. 1–10).

Stories of David
The youngest chosen (I Samuel xvi. 1–12).
The lion and the bear (I Samuel xvii. 32–37).
Goliath (I Samuel xvii. 1–51).
Naaman's little maid (II Kings v. 1–14).

The Friends of Jesus
Martha and Mary (St Luke x. 38–42).
The disciples (St Luke vi. 12–17; St Mark i. 14–20; ii. 13–17;
St John i. 35–51, xv. 11–17).
The centurion (St Luke vii. 1–10).

Stories told by Jesus in His teaching
The sower (St Mark iv. 1–9, 13–20).
The seed growing secretly (St Mark iv. 26–29).
The mustard seed (St Mark iv. 30–32).
The house on the rock (St Matthew vii. 24–27).
The parables in Luke xv with Psalm xxiii.
The treasure-finder (St Matthew xiii. 44).
Forgiveness (St Matthew xviii. 21–35).

Kind deeds of Jesus
> The children (St Mark x. 13-16).
> The palsied man (St Luke v. 18-26).
> At the pool of Bethesda (St John v. 2-9).
> Jairus' daughter (St Mark v. 21-24 and 35-43).
> Zacchaeus (St Luke xix. 1-10).

Stories of the Followers of Jesus

Many teachers will have their own collection of stories of saints, missionary heroes and others, both ancient and modern, who have been followers of Jesus. The names suggested below are a few of those in whose lives there were incidents which provide suitable lesson material. Their stories can be found in the books mentioned in the Book List on pp. 175-176; these books also give many other suitable stories, and teachers should feel free to make their own selection. Children of this age will enjoy making little books of their own about the various people in the stories. They can also be encouraged to find extra material from home; this can be the beginning of their search for sources, which, if rightly fostered, will be invaluable later.

> Dorcas (Acts ix. 36-39). St Gregory and St Augustine.
> St Francis. St Patrick. St Nicholas.
> St Christopher. St Columba. Mary Slessor.
> St Martin. St Cuthbert. David Livingstone.

THE JUNIOR SCHOOL

CHILDREN AGED 7-11

From the age of seven to the age of eleven a child's horizon is continually widening; for his society he requires more than the intimate circle provided by home and family; for his interests he demands a larger world than satisfied his needs before. During this period, usually in the first half of it, he passes from delight in the fanciful to pre-occupation with the real; in the transition he demands sometimes one, sometimes the other. He passes from childishness and the need for security to robustness and a desire for independence. By the time the 'upper Junior' stage is reached, the normal child is a vigorous young creature, feeling his power as an individual and wanting plenty of outlet for an active mind and body. He is interested in people, and in his daily life, in stories and in books, he is looking for heroes he can admire.

For these reasons the stories chosen from the Old Testament, and the stories of saints, martyrs and missionary heroes, are particularly suitable at this stage of development. In the Old Testament stories the events move quickly; they contain plenty of action and are rich in picturesque detail. They are about men and women who *do* things and have great adventures. Above all they are about men and women to whom God was the greatest reality, however rudimentary and undeveloped their ideas about Him may have been. The heroes of the early Hebrews, sometimes savage and primitive, appeal to the young child who is often a little savage himself. And, if he takes for granted their brutality, he can follow them, with unexpected spiritual insight, in their greatest deeds and thoughts. But in order that the person of Jesus shall remain throughout at the centre of all the teaching, these stories from the Old Testament, in the 'lower Junior' stage at any rate, should be introduced as 'Stories Told to Jesus'. If this method of introduction is considered too childish for the 'upper Junior' stage, the Old Testament stories should be approached as part of the preparation for the coming of Jesus. The stories of the later followers of Jesus are particularly important in relating the religious teaching to the children's lives, and in avoiding giving the impression that religion is something which only belongs to the 'Ever so long ago'.

With the Old Testament stories the question 'Is it true?' will surely arise. The child in the Infant School has already begun to ask it, and the Junior continues to ask it insistently. This familiar difficulty can only be met adequately if two distinctions are clearly held in the mind of the teacher.

The first distinction lies in the difference between history and what is considered to be myth or legend. A 'Myth' is a story which makes no claim to relate actual historical facts, but has a symbolic meaning. Myths are usually designed to give an explanation of the mysteries of Nature and of human life. In the Old Testament the stories of Eden and the Fall, of Noah's Ark and the Tower of Babel can be regarded as myths.

A 'Legend', on the other hand, has some relation to historical fact. In many cases a dim memory of very ancient happenings has been transformed in being handed down through the medium of folk tales; this is what has happened in the case of some of the Patriarchal stories. In other cases, events substantially historical have been imaginatively embroidered. A child can be led to understand how the legend grew. Such are some of the stories about Elijah and Elisha. The hero kings and leaders are really historical characters, but their stories are often largely legendary. In considerable portions, however, of the Books of Samuel and Kings we are on strictly historical ground. (In this connection, the 'Note on History, Legend and Myth', p. 143, should be carefully studied.)

The distinction between history, legend and myth should ever be in the mind of the teacher, and should affect the manner in which the stories of the Old Testament are told. Such an awareness will assist in the making of the second distinction necessary to answer the question 'Is it true?' This distinction is constituted by the difference between spiritual or moral truth and the truth of historical fact. These are not hostile to each other, but complementary. There is truth of the kind which narrates historical fact; but there is also the truth which a writer can best express by symbolising it in a story. In the latter case one must not look for a truth of historical fact which the story does not claim; nor must the particulars of the story be allowed to obscure the general truth conveyed.

The artist, the poet, the prophet—all have their vision of reality and employ their own peculiar means of conveying it to others. The truth to which their insight gives testimony is not subject to the yardsticks of scientific measurement or the verification of proven occurrence. The spirit of Man recognises that there are realms of reality intuitively attained in which the laws of science and the canons of history are not transgressed but are transcended. We do not pretend that the details of the Genesis story of the Creation agree exactly with the scientifically discovered 'facts' of geology and astronomy concerning the history of the universe, but this does not invalidate the assertion of Genesis that God created the world.

In the Gospels and Acts we are in the main in contact with actual historical reminiscence. Here the central figure is the centre of our faith and teaching. The children will hear stories of Him as a Child, Man, Friend, Leader, Healer and Saviour. The stories of Christmas and Easter will be told, of course, as the festivals come round. It is a pity to tell them every time exactly as they stand in the Bible; for some children when they hear the same account again and again, are inclined to think they know all about it, when probably they are only just beginning to understand its significance. It is sometimes good to look at the events from a different angle, telling the story of the Passion, for example, as it would be seen through the eyes of the centurion (cf. John Masefield's *Good Friday*), or the Christmas story as seen by the shepherds. The longer narrative of the Passion and the events leading up to it, should be reserved for the fourth year, when the children of 10–11 will be better able to understand it. The telling of the miracle stories will probably evoke the question 'How did it happen?' If full explanation is not desirable at this stage, we may simply have to say: 'That is the story as told by one of Jesus' disciples.' (In this connection, the Note on 'Miracles' on p. 148 will be found helpful.)

And what of the method of teaching? Some of the stories in the Old Testament have an impressive simplicity and grandeur, while the stories and parables from the New Testament are incomparable. At first the teacher should not read them but tell them, and tell them really well. But the child must play his part; indeed, he is ready for as much activity as we can give him. He will take part in the dramatisation of stories with zest. Then there is illustration. What child, after hearing the stories of Joseph and his brethren, is not ready to seize colour and make a picture in which that coat of many colours is given the prominence befitting such a picturesque garment?

Learning by heart has its place, provided that it is not made a long and monotonous task; and this can be avoided by choral speaking in unison, and by the arrangement of the class into a speech choir, whereby variations of emphasis and changes of speaker can be clearly marked, and an antiphonal arrangement followed if suitable. (The teacher is advised to consult the Note on 'Making the Bible Familiar to Children' on p. 140.)

There will be many opportunities for handwork in connection with Bible stories, either as separate pieces of work or as parts of a larger project. This project method offers great scope to the teacher who knows how to use it. There is no reason why projects using puppets should not be used in connection with Bible stories. Great care must be exercised in the choice of pictures used. (Guidance on this is given in the Note on 'The Artist and the Christian Faith', p. 152.) There are many illustrated books of reference for children, and the daily newspaper often furnishes news and illustrations of the findings of archaeologists. Film strips can be of great assistance, particularly with the 'background' material, by depicting clothes, customs and architecture different from those familiar to the children. Films may be useful for the same purpose, but the number of good religious films is at present small.

The Morning Assembly is an integral part of the Religious Teaching of the school, and offers great possibilities for fostering a spirit of friendliness and genuine religious feeling, and for an introduction to the practice of worship. Perhaps there is need for more formality than was found desirable in the Infant classes, but an unvaried form of service is undesirable and tends to grow meaningless through being repeated mechanically day by day.

Hymn singing should always be enjoyed, but the tunes should be really good ones, the words sensible and not sentimental. The prayers, again, should be chosen for their appropriateness and for the simplicity and beauty of their language. Some should be so simple that after hearing them several times, the children will be able to say them themselves. Others should be more difficult and challenging. Children who can read well should be included in those who read the lesson, which should not be too long. Children will learn simple responses just by hearing them as part of the service. They enjoy writing out their own services, including their favourite hymns and prayers, and these should sometimes be used. But the chief thing is that the Assembly should be spontaneous and alive, the children really taking part, and not listening to something imposed—and we would almost say that it should never be quite the same two days together.

Note. The Bible references given throughout the whole of this section are meant primarily for the teacher, and are not always suitable for the children. It is intended that teachers should build up lessons, a lesson or part of a lesson on the subject suggested, using the Biblical reference in whatever way suits the plan of the lesson best.

The planning of the Junior Syllabus in two parts, that for children aged 7–9, and that for children aged 9–11, is intended to leave head teachers free to make their own arrangement of the material in each two-year course in the way which suits their school best. A result of setting out the Syllabus in this manner is that all the Old Testament material for two years is naturally grouped together, but it should not therefore be supposed that the Old Testament sections are indivisible units which must be regarded as continuous blocks of teaching. It is for the head teacher to decide how the material is best portioned out to suit his school's particular requirements and at the same time to preserve the balance of the whole.

CHILDREN AGED 7–9

I. THE CHILDHOOD OF JESUS

The Gospels tell us very little of the childhood of Jesus. The teacher can draw upon the background material available to build up a picture of the type of life led by the ordinary Jewish child in the Palestine of Jesus' day. The stories which were told to Jesus form an introduction to the Old Testament.

Bedtime Stories told to Jesus by His Mother

In connection with these stories the teacher is recommended to consult the Note on 'History, Legend and Myth' on p. 143.

> God's garden (Genesis ii).
> The forbidden fruit (Genesis iii).
> Noah's ark (Genesis vi. 9–ix. 17).
> Moses the hidden baby (Exodus i. 7–ii. 10).
> The boy Samuel (I Samuel i; ii. 18, 19, 26; iii. 1–10, 15–21).
> David the shepherd—introducing Psalm xxiii and the songs which Jesus learned. (Other suitable Psalms: c, cvii, cl.)
> David and Goliath (I Samuel xvii).

Jesus at School: stories of the Early Hebrews in their life and work

The only books in a Jewish school of Jesus' day were those of the Bible of the time—the rolls of the various books of 'the Law', 'the Prophets' and 'the Writings', which together comprise our 'Old Testament'.

The early stories of the Hebrews show them in their home life, their work and travel. They will be appreciated for their own worth; but at the same time, if they are skilfully told and good illustrations are used, the teacher can give a picture of the country and of the conditions under which these pastoral people lived, which will serve as a background to the later Old Testament stories and history.

> Abraham: his call and journey (Genesis xii. 1–10).
>   Parting from Lot (Genesis xiii).
> Isaac and Rebekah (Genesis xxiv).
> Jacob and Esau (Genesis xxv. 20–34; xxvii, 1–45).
>   Jacob's ladder (Genesis xxviii. 1–7, 10–22).
>   Rachel (Genesis xxix. 1–20).
>   Reunion with Esau (Genesis xxxii. 1–21; xxxiii).
> Joseph and his brethren (Genesis xxxvii).
>   In Egypt (Genesis xxxix. 1–6, 20–23).
>   In prison (Genesis xl).
>   Interprets Pharaoh's dreams and is made ruler (Genesis xli).

The coming of his brethren (Genesis xlii–xlv).
The coming of the Israelites into Egypt (Genesis xlvii. 1–7, 28–31; xlviii. 1–12).
Ruth and Naomi (Ruth i, ii, iv. 13–17).

The Boy Jesus in the Temple

What Jesus had learnt at home and at school made Him ask many questions which neither His mother nor His teachers could answer. As soon as He had the chance, He went to learn more from those who were wiser. (Luke ii. 40–52.)

Stories from Jesus' Bible

Before beginning the story of Moses the teacher will explain how the Hebrews had dwelt in Egypt for a long time, how they had multiplied, and how the descendants of the Pharaoh who had given them the land of Goshen had enslaved them. Moses is the slaves' champion and deliverer.

It has been thought wiser to omit the account of the plagues. As the account stands, it suggests a view of the character and activity of God which cannot be accepted as true; a God who is willing to kill all the first-born of one nation so that another may be released is a cruel and arbitrary God. If, on the other hand, the story is rationalised and the plagues are treated as natural events, their real meaning is equally misinterpreted. In the passages selected the story moves from Moses contending with the magicians of Egypt to the Passover and the hasty flight.

Moses—the Hero of Faith
    Childhood; flight from Egypt (Exodus i, ii).
    Sojourn in the land of Midian; the burning bush (Exodus iii).
    In Egypt; hardness of Pharaoh (Exodus vii, 1–13).
    Going out of Egypt (Exodus xii. 1–11; xiii. 17–22; xiv; xv. 20–27).
    In the wilderness (Exodus xvi, xviii).
    Mount Sinai (Exodus xxiv. 12–18; xxxi. 18).
    The golden calf (Exodus xxxii. 1–20, 26).
    Making the Ark (Exodus xxxvii. 1–5; Numbers x. 33–36).
    The people complain (Numbers xi. 4–9, 31–32; xx. 1–11).

The promised land (Deuteronomy viii. 1–14).
The death of Moses (Deuteronomy xxxiv).

Soldier Leaders
Joshua; crossing the Jordan (Joshua iii. 5–8, 13–17).
The fall of Jericho (Joshua ii, vi).
Deborah—heroine and liberator (Judges iv).
Gideon and the valiant three hundred (Judges vi. 11–40
vii. 1–23).
Samson—a strong man and his weakness (Judges xiv. 5–20;
xvi. 2–31).

II. JESUS IN HIS RELATIONS WITH HIS PEOPLE

Scenes from the Gospels, in which Jesus is shown in contact with various types of people, are used to bring out His character and personality. The primary aim is to give examples of the way in which Jesus dealt with people. No attempt is made to arrange the material chronologically. The miracle stories are introduced, primarily, as examples of the compassion and authority of Jesus at work in response to human need.

Stories from the lives of Saints and other great Christians who have been inspired by Jesus' attitude to these different classes of people are used to show how courageous men and women in all ages have tried to follow His example. The names given in brackets are only suggestions; other suitable names will occur to the teacher, who will also be able to find appropriate stories about recent events and living people.

Jesus and the Children
Blessing the children (St Mark x. 13–16).
Receiving the children (St Mark ix. 33–37).
The Nobleman's son (St John iv. 46–53).
[Dr Barnardo.]

Jesus and the Poor
The widow's mite (St Mark xii. 41–44).
Blind Bartimaeus (St Mark x. 46–52).
[Charles Kingsley and *The Water-Babies*, Lord Shaftesbury.]

Jesus and the Sick

> The paralytic (St Mark ii. 1–12).
> The crippled woman (St Luke xiii. 10–17).
> The man with the withered hand (St Matthew xii. 9–13).
>
> (In the apocryphal Gospel according to the Hebrews the man says 'I was a bricklayer, earning my living with my hands. I beseech thee, Jesus, restore my health to me, that I may not be disgraced by begging bread.')
> [Florence Nightingale.]

Jesus and the Outcast

> The lepers (St Luke xvii. 11–19).
> The Syrophenician woman (St Mark vii. 24–30).
> [Father Damien, Elizabeth Fry.]

Jesus and His Friends

> The first disciples (St Mark i. 16–20).
> Mary, Martha and Lazarus (St Mark xiv. 3–9; St Luke x. 38, 39; St John xi. 5).
> Washing the disciples' feet (St John xiii. 1–17).
> [St Francis of Assisi.]

III. JESUS AS TEACHER

Parables told by Jesus

For work on the Parables the teacher is referred to the suggestions on p. 22 in the Introduction to the Section and to the Note on 'Making the Bible Familiar to Children' on p. 140. The Parables with their dramatic qualities and the wealth of realistic detail, suggested though not always expressed in the text, lend themselves particularly well to children's acting. The telling of the stories will occupy a comparatively short time, but they can be acted, and acted again, with increasing use of detail. The detail must be supplied by the teacher from the books of reference[1] or by the children themselves from such books as *Bible Books for Small People*. If the children's imagination supplies further detail, this will enhance the value of the stories for them. As the list of

---

[1] The teacher is recommended to consult the List of Books for Reference, especially the section on 'Biblical Background' on p. 163.

stories grows, other activities will suggest themselves, such as finding the memorable verses in each one, finding how many of them refer to country things, how many to parties and social life, which are the joyful ones and which are the sad. At the end of the term the children should not only have enjoyed many stories, they should also have become familiar with Jesus' way of talking to simple people, His feeling for them and thoughts about them, and they should have resumed and extended their acquaintance with the life of His time and country.

The sower (St Mark iv. 3–20).
Weeds in the corn (St Matthew xiii. 24–30).
The mustard seed (St Matthew xiii. 31–32).
The house upon a rock (St Matthew vii. 24–27).
The unfruitful fig tree (St Luke xiii. 6–9).
The Good Samaritan (St Luke x. 25–37).
Visitors at night (St Luke xi. 5–8).
The talents (St Matthew xxv. 14–30).
The lost sheep (St Luke xv. 3–7).
The lost coin (St Luke xv. 8–10).
The Prodigal Son (St Luke xv. 11–32).
The Pharisee and the Publican (St Luke xviii. 9–14).
The unforgiving debtor (St Matthew xviii. 23–35).
Invitation to a feast (St Luke xiv. 7–14).
The great supper (St Luke xiv. 16–24).
The foolish virgins (St Matthew xxv. 1–13).

IV. SOME STORIES OF PETER

It is not intended in this section to give anything approaching a biography of Peter. A number of the more dramatic incidents in his life have been chosen; from these can be built up a picture of the man into whose care above all others Jesus committed the continuation of His work.

Meeting with Jesus (St John i. 35–42).
His call (St Mark i. 16–18).
Jesus in Peter's house (St Matthew viii. 14–15).
Walking on the water (St Matthew xiv. 22–33).
In the garden (St Luke xxii. 39–53; St John xviii. 10–11).

The denial (St Luke xxii. 31–34, 54–62).
At the sepulchre (St John xx. 1–10).
By the Sea of Galilee (St John xxi. 1–22).
Pentecost (Acts ii).
Healing the lame man (Acts iii).
Arrest and acquittal (Acts iv).
Imprisonment and escape (Acts xii. 1–17).

CHILDREN AGED 9–11

I. THE LIFE OF JESUS

It is suggested that at this stage some attempt should be made to give a first impression of what may be described as the drama of the Life and Death of Jesus. The continuous study of the life is postponed to a later stage. Here are selected some salient episodes which suggest the character and work of Jesus as a Saviour, and the conflict which issued in His death and the final triumph of the Resurrection. John the Baptist proclaims the coming Saviour. Jesus at His baptism is designated as Saviour. In the Temptation He accepts and defines His mission. His ministry is introduced with the proclamation 'The Kingdom of God is at hand'. A period of public preaching arouses the opposition of the Pharisees and ends with the choice of His disciples. The mission of the disciples illustrates the proclamation of the Kingdom of God in word and deed. The feeding of the multitude with its sequel is treated as the central crisis of the ministry. Afterwards Jesus in retirement (almost flight) is acknowledged as Saviour by His disciples, and He tells them what it means to follow Him. The triumphal entry is the public manifestation of His claim, and the cleansing of the temple challenges the authorities. The Council of the Jewish elders replies by a conspiracy with Judas. Jesus institutes the Last Supper, and the same night is betrayed. The narrative of the Passion, Death and Resurrection is then given somewhat fully.

The preaching of John the Baptist (St Matthew iii. 4–12).
The baptism of Jesus (St Mark i. 9–11).
The temptation (St Matthew iv. 1–11).
The proclamation of the Gospel (St Mark i. 14–15).

Hostility aroused by:
  Breaking the Sabbath (St Luke vi. 1–11; xiv. 1–6).
  Consorting with publicans and sinners (St Luke vii. 36–50;
                                             xix. 1–10).
  His claims (St Mark ii. 1–12).
A new teaching (St Mark i. 21–28; St Luke x. 25–37; xv).
Appointing the Twelve (St Luke vi. 12–16).
The mission (St Mark vi. 7–13; St Luke x. 1–12, 17).
Rejection at Nazareth (St Matthew xiii. 54–58).
Feeding the multitude; attempt to make Jesus king (St
                                             John vi. 1–15).
Retirement (St Matthew xv. 21).
Peter's confession (St Mark viii. 27–38).
The Transfiguration (St Luke ix. 28–36).
Secret return to Galilee; blessing the children (St Mark ix.
                                             30–37; x. 13–16).
The journey to Jerusalem (St Matthew xx. 17–19).
The triumphal entry (St Mark xi. 1–11).
The cleansing of the Temple (St Mark xi. 15–19).
The conspiracy (St John xi. 47–53; St Mark xiv.1–2, 10–11).
The Last Supper (St Mark xiv. 12–31)
The arrest (St Mark xiv. 32–52).
Peter's denial (St Luke xxii. 54–62).
The trial before Pilate (St Mark xv. 1–15).
The Crucifixion (St Mark xv. 16–39).
The Empty Tomb (St Mark xvi. 1–8).
Jesus and Mary Magdalene (St John xx. 11–18).
Emmaus (St Luke xxiv. 13–35).
Jesus by the Sea of Galilee (St John xxi).

II. OLD TESTAMENT

Children have already been introduced to the Old Testament
through 'Stories Jesus Heard'. They will now be able to become
more familiar with it as the 'Bible' which Jesus knew and which
he heard read every Sabbath in the Synagogue. They may also
become more familiar with the Book of Psalms as the hymn-book
Jesus used. The following are suggested as being suitable for
reading or learning by heart at any time during the two years'

course. They may be learnt in their Bible form or in Coverdale's version made familiar by the Book of Common Prayer.

Psalm xv.	Lord, who shall abide in thy tabernacle?
xxiii.	The Lord is my shepherd.
xxiv.	The earth is the Lord's.
xlvi.	God is our refuge.
lxxxiv.	How amiable are thy tabernacles.
xci.	He that dwelleth in the secret place of the most High.
ciii.	Bless the Lord, O my soul.
cxvii.	O praise the Lord.
cxxi.	I will lift up mine eyes unto the hills.
cxlviii.	Praise ye the Lord.

The Early Kings

Up to the time of Samuel, the only king of the Israelites had been God, who had led them by means of his spokesmen, such as Moses and Samuel. It was then felt that the Israelites would have greater strength to maintain themselves against the heathen Philistines if they were organised into a kingdom under the central control of a royal commander-in-chief. But it was necessary to be sure that the new king was a man chosen by God, and that the Israelites, now that they had a king, should never forget that their supreme ruler was still God.

Here the early rulers are shown as men and heroes, and the references have been selected to include the best stories of their achievements and to show the different sides of their characters. They all had great human failings and imperfections, but their leadership did help to consolidate the position of the Israelites, and their worship of God, in the midst of a turbulent, pagan world.

Samuel (I Samuel i. 9–28; ii; iii. 1–12, 15–20).
Saul is chosen Israel's first king (I Samuel ix; x. 14–24).
Saul and David
    Saul forfeits his kingdom (I Samuel xv. 22–23; xvi).
    David slays Goliath (I Samuel xvii).
    David's friendship with Jonathan, and Saul's jealousy
                (I Samuel xviii, 1–16; xix. 1–16; xx).

David spares Saul's life (I Samuel xxiv).

The death of Saul and his sons (I Samuel xxxi).

The news brought to David (II Samuel i).

David proclaimed king (II Samuel v. 1–5).

His kindness (II Samuel iv. 4; ix).

His sin; 'Thou art the man' (II Samuel xi. 1–3, 14–17, 26–27; xii. 1–10).

The revolt and death of Absalom (II Samuel xv. 1–6, 10–14; xviii).

David names his successor (I Kings i. 1, 28–40; ii. 1–4, 10).

Solomon asks for wisdom (I Kings iii. 1–15).

His wisdom as a judge (I Kings iii. 16–28).

The building and dedication of the temple (I Kings v; vi. 7; vii. 51; viii. 1, 12–24).

The Queen of Sheba (I Kings x. 1–13).

Solomon compromises with heathenism, and his government becomes oppressive (I Kings xi. 1–10; v. 13–17; xii. 4).

Division of the kingdom (I Kings xi. 41–43; xii. 1–24).

Prophets in Israel

Dramatic incidents and vivid prophecy have been chosen from the lives of the prophets. They can be told (and dramatised), quite simply, as the stories of brave men who were not afraid to denounce the evils of their time and who looked forward to a day of greater righteousness.

Elijah

Fed by the ravens (I Kings xvii. 1–7).

The widow's cruse (I Kings xvii. 8–16).

Healing the woman's son (I Kings xvii. 17–24).

Confounding the prophets of Baal (I Kings xviii. 1–39).

Under the juniper tree (I Kings xix. 1–8).

'The still small voice' (I Kings xix. 9–18).

The mantle of Elijah (I Kings xix. 19–21).

Naboth's vineyard (I Kings xxi).

The death of Ahab (I Kings xxii. 1–40).

Elisha

The chariot of fire (II Kings ii. 1–15).

The little room (II Kings iv. 8–11).
The widow's child (II Kings iv. 12–37).
The captive maid (II Kings v).

Amos
Protests against the wicked rich (Amos vi. 1–6; viii. 4–8).
Prophet against priest (Amos vii. 10–17).

Isaiah
His call (Isaiah vi. 1–8).
Sennacherib (Isaiah xxxvi; xxxvii).

The Northern Kingdom falls (II Kings xvii).

Josiah's reformation (II Kings xxii; xxiii. 1–8).

Jeremiah
The good and bad figs (Jeremiah xxiv).
The king's penknife (Jeremiah xxxvi. 9–32).
Cast into the dungeon (Jeremiah xxxviii).

Exile in Babylon
Jerusalem taken (II Kings xxv. 1–4, 8–10).
The captivity (Psalm cxxxvii; Jeremiah xxix. 1–14).

Daniel [1]
The Golden Image (Daniel iii. 1–19).
Saved from the fiery furnace (Daniel iii. 20–30).
Nebuchadnezzar's dream (Daniel iv).
The writing on the wall (Daniel v).
In the lions' den (Daniel vi).

Cyrus permits the Return (II Chronicles xxxvi. 22–23).

III. SOME STORIES OF PAUL

An attempt has been made to get away from the stereotyped way of presenting Paul's life in terms of missionary journeys. The episodes selected are meant to bring out his character and to give the child a sense of his achievements.

Stephen (Acts vii. 54–viii. 1).
The road to Damascus (Acts ix. 1–9).
Saul at Damascus (Acts ix. 10–27).

[1] The Book of Daniel was written approximately 400 years later, but tells stories of the time of the Exile.

Paul and Barnabas work together (Acts xiii. 1–4, 14–16, 42–52).

Jupiter and Mercury (Acts xiv. 6–20).

The man of Macedonia (Acts xvi. 6–10).

The slave girl of Philippi (Acts xvi. 11–24).

The jailor (Acts xvi. 25–40).

'Another king, one Jesus' (Acts xvii. 1–9).

Tent-making at Corinth (Acts xviii. 1–4).

Gallio (Acts xviii. 12–17).

The riot in the theatre (Acts xix. 23–41).

Sleeping during the sermon (Acts xx. 7–12).

Danger ahead (Acts xxi. 1–15).

Protective arrest (Acts xxi. 27–39).

Paul's defence (Acts xxii. 1–21).

The Roman citizen (Acts xxii. 22–30).

The plot (Acts xiii. 11–35).

The appeal to Caesar (Acts xxv. 1–12).

The shipwreck (Acts xxvii).

Malta (Acts xxviii. 1–10).

The road to Rome (Acts xxviii. 11–16).

IV. FOLLOWERS OF JESUS

Stories from the lives of Saints and other great Christians show how Jesus has inspired men and women to follow Him in all ages. It is probably better to intersperse these stories with the rest of the course rather than to take them as a continuous block of teaching, it being left to the teacher to choose the appropriate point at which to introduce a given story.

Many teachers will be familiar with a large number of suitable stories, but the following suggestions may be useful. The list is not exhaustive or exclusive; there are many books available which give this type of material in convenient form. (A number are mentioned in the Book List on p. 175.)

The Forty Martyrs of Sebaste.	William Carey.
Bede.	Bishop Patterson.
Ignatius Loyola.	Khama.
John Bunyan.	Captain Oates.

William Penn.   Bishop Selwyn.
Booker Washington.   Lister.
Sadhu Sundar Singh.   Pasteur.
David Livingstone.   Albert Schweitzer.

PRAYER

Teachers have a great opportunity to help children to learn something of the art of prayer. It is left to head teachers to decide at what stage it will suit their school best for this section of the course to be taken. While care should be taken not to force upon children ideas about prayer too advanced for their years, it is nevertheless important to convey to children that prayer is something more than asking God for what we want. It should be possible to express in simple words that it is a placing of the self at the disposal of God—which can be illustrated from Gethsemane. Without checking the child's instinct to ask God for things (since this is an expression of his reliance on God, and, as such, is prayer in the true sense), the teacher can show him other and higher forms of prayer. The step from petition to intercession is not difficult. The child can be assured of forgiveness for his sins if, without dwelling on them in any morbid fashion, he confesses them to God and is genuinely sorry for them. He can be led to recapture the spirit of wondering adoration which was natural in earlier years; one approach to this can be made through thanksgiving. As a child realises for what he has to thank God he will come imperceptibly to praise and adore. Reference should also be made to the section on 'Religion in the School' on pp. 10–15.

The child should be helped to face the need for discipline in prayer, and the practical difficulties, such as that of securing time and privacy. As the child is shown Jesus at prayer, he may be taught the times and manner appropriate to his own prayer.

The teacher will wish to ensure that prayer is no 'vain repetition': to this end children should be encouraged to make up their own prayers; other simple ones can be given, it being explained that they are for the children's own use: making a book of these will provide suitable expression work. The question of 'unanswered prayer' is sure to arise; while it can be indicated that it is the life of prayer which is answered, not the occasional invocation, children can also be shown that they themselves can have a share in the fulfilment of their prayers; this can be illustrated from the story of the sick man carried to Jesus by his friends. It can further be pointed out that no prayer ever really goes unanswered —it is we who fail to recognise a negative answer, the wisdom of which is at the time hidden from us.

Jesus at Prayer

Early in the morning (St Mark i. 35).
In the mountains (St Mark vi. 46).
Before choosing the Apostles (St Luke vi. 12–13).
Grace before meat (St Luke ix. 16).
The Great Thanksgiving (St Luke x. 21–22).
In the garden (St Matthew xxvi. 36–44).

Jesus teaches His disciples to pray

The disciples' request (St Luke xi. 1).
After this manner (St Luke xi. 2–4).
Ask and ye shall receive (St Luke xi. 5–13).
In quietness and simplicity (St Matthew vi. 5–8).

Petition

Solomon prays for wisdom (I Kings iii. 5–15).
The King's sickness (II Kings xx. 1–5).
A selfish prayer (St Mark x. 35–40).
The leper (St Matthew viii. 2–3).

Intercession

The man carried by his friends (St Luke v. 18–20).
The Centurion (St Luke vii. 1–10).
The Syrophenician woman (St Mark vii. 25–30).
St Peter (Acts xii. 5–17).
For the sick (James v. 14–15).
(Some reference can be made to Jesus' prayer for His followers contained in St John xvii.)

Confession

The Pharisee and the Publican (St Luke xviii. 9–14).
The Prodigal Son (St Luke xv. 11–32).

Thanksgiving

   The Magnificat (St Luke i. 46–55).
   The Song of Simeon (St Luke ii. 25–32).
   Hosanna (St Mark xi. 1–10).
   The lepers (St Luke xvii. 11–19).

Adoration

   Isaiah in the temple (Isaiah vi. 1–3).
   The Wise Men (St Matthew ii. 1–11).
   The Angels (St Luke ii. 8–14).
   The whole company of Heaven (Revelation vii. 9–12).

THE SECONDARY SCHOOL

CHILDREN AGED 11–16

Up to the age of eleven a child has been told Old Testament stories without any attempt being made to piece them together as a consecutive history. He has now reached the age when he can begin to grasp the significance of historical events. From stories heard in the Junior course, he is familiar with the names of prophets and kings in the Old Testament, and many of the events of the history of the Israelites will not be new. It should now be possible to recapitulate and draw together all this material into a coherent account. The record contained in the Old Testament is often taught merely as Jewish history—even if it is the history of the chosen people guided by God. But it is more than the history of a chosen people; it is also a record of the development of ideas concerning Man and God, the relationship between them, and how man should live and behave. Using the historical background as the canvas, it will be possible in the later part of the course to trace in outline the development of these religious ideas through the Old Testament up to their culmination in the life and teaching of Jesus.

During this period of early adolescence the child is growing towards young manhood and beginning to realise something of what he can do with his life. Once interested in himself almost entirely objectively, he is now thinking of himself in relation to others and to God. With puberty comes self-consciousness and the dawn of the idealism of later adolescence. This then is the time to present the picture of the Ideal Personality through the records of our Lord's life. The main concern of this period should be to arrive at a complete picture of a real man, the Jesus of Nazareth who knew hunger, weariness and danger; who could be grieved and angry as well as patient and tender, merry as well as compassionate; who could pierce men's hypocrisy and disguises, and who showed men what life at its highest could be. The Ideal Personality and the Perfect Leader might demand no more from the child than hero-worship, a bright enough flame while it lasts but bound to flicker out. But Christ is more than a hero to be admired, He is the revelation of God in history, and an abiding power in the lives of men. It is for this latter reason that stories are included in the course showing this power throughout the centuries right down to the present day, in the lives of men and women for whom He was 'the Way, the Truth and the Life'.

Method is largely a matter for the decision of the individual teacher. Many means which have been found successful in other teaching can be applied to religious instruction as well. While there is still room for story-telling, classes should be encouraged to discuss and debate, to make their own discoveries from 'original sources'; our Lord's motives for such a saying as 'See thou tell no man' might be discussed; while the attitude of the Pharisees might be 'discovered' from references in a given Gospel. There is a place for memory work, if the methods outlined on pp. 141–143 are adopted and mere mechanical repetition is avoided. Good pictures, picture-making, film-strips and other visual aids will still play their part. It has been recognised that some children will probably be unable to follow the standard course, and to meet their needs special suggestions have been made.

While the teacher should teach, and not preach, in the classroom, he should have an ever-present sense of responsibility that by his teaching the children may be 'led into the way of truth'. Whether by the direct, positive story method, used most with backward children, or by the more strictly 'ethical' approach possible with intelligent pupils, some indication can be given of the simple, essential things of the Christian life—faith in God the Father, Creator and Preserver; love of Jesus Christ 'who came to show us how to live'; reverence for what is noble; desire for goodness; readiness for self-sacrifice; an attitude of worship springing from a sense of dependence, wonder and gratitude; and a realisation of the need for consideration and respect for others, which is the foundation of corporate life. The teacher has a unique opportunity for conveying these things. But all his explanations of them will be vain if he does not display them, however unostentatiously, in his own living. 'It is the sincere word, not the clever one, which is most likely to make the poor sounds of the human voice the vehicle of grace.' (INGE.)

Note. The planning of the Syllabus for children aged 11–15 in two parts, that for children aged 11–13, and that for children aged 13–15, is intended to leave head teachers free to make their own arrangement of the material in each two-year course in the way which suits their school best. A result of setting out the Syllabus in this manner is that all the Old Testament material for two years is naturally grouped together, but it should not therefore be supposed that the Old Testament sections are indivisible units which must be regarded as continuous blocks of teaching. It is for the head teacher to decide how the material is best portioned out to suit his school's particular requirements and at the same time preserve the balance of the whole.

CHILDREN AGED 11–13

I. THE LIFE OF CHRIST

In the study of the life of Jesus based on St Mark's Gospel and Acts i–iv, the intention is to draw together into an integrated whole, all the parables, miracles and stories of Jesus with which the children have become acquainted in the Junior stage.

A penetrating study of Jesus' teaching is not here proposed. This is reserved for the later stage of adolescence, where questions of conduct and problems about God are more naturally of interest and concern. The aim here should be to present as complete a picture as possible of Jesus as a person, and to give reality to the portrait. Probably this can best be done by bringing out the dramatic quality of His life and death. The drama as a whole is that of the coming and reception of a Saviour, a Deliverer, a Messiah, and through it run three main threads.

The first thread concerns Jesus' own conception of His mission and the methods He was to employ. We know little about the life of Jesus before He began His ministry. We have one glimpse of Him at the age of twelve, which reveals Him even at this early age intensely concerned with religious questions. He did not begin His ministry until He was about thirty. What were His thoughts and ponderings during the preceding years? We are not told; but one can be certain that the messages of the Old Testament must have been much in His mind. Then there were the ideas current in His day concerning a Messiah. The story of Jesus as told in the Gospel assumes throughout that He appeared as 'Messiah' (or in Greek, 'Christ'). The Messiah had become in Jewish thought of the first century an ideal figure expected to appear upon the stage of history as the representative of God to fulfil His purposes for His people. With His coming the Reign (or Kingdom) of God would come; that is to say, God, the invisible King of all the world, would exert His power directly and manifestly to overcome the powers of evil and give His people a blessed life in communion with Him. The Gospel makes it clear that Jesus fulfilled God's purpose for His people, though not in the manner which most people expected, since the hope of the Messiah generally sprang from the Jews' desire for political freedom.

In considering His Ministry, Jesus had to face the same kind of temptations as all human beings meet, temptations to satisfy immediate physical cravings, or desires for personal power and position, before consulting God's will. In the case of Jesus these temptations had a particular force when He came to choose the method by which He was to carry out His mission. In order to be able to face these temptations away from the distractions of everyday life, Jesus wrestled with them 'in the wilderness'. The story of His temptation is fundamental to the whole drama of His life and work.

Should He re-establish an independent kingdom of the Jews, in place of the client kingdom of Herod, who, in spite of his ostentatious temple-building, knew little of true religion and collaborated with the heathen overlords of Rome? Should He restore the temporal power of the Jewish nation to the boundaries it had known in the great days of Solomon? Should He thereby prove that God was still 'the Lord of Hosts' whose strong right arm would demonstrate conclusively His guidance of His chosen people, as in the days of old, in further fulfilment of the Covenant He had made? It was an attractive idea; it would be a purpose readily understood by the people, to throw the Romans back into the sea and be rid of their hated taxes. Furthermore, there was an instrument ready to hand for the purpose—the political party of the Zealots, whose very aim this was. All He had to do was to declare Himself their God-appointed Leader. In spite of the obvious appeal of such a course, He could not reconcile it with the best teaching of the Old Testament, especially the latter part of the Book of Isaiah, nor with His reading of Jewish history. In the early days God had indeed guided His people to political independence in order that their worship of the one true God might not be contaminated by the paganism of other nations. But if that was all, if that was the end of the story, why had He permitted the Exile? And the Roman domination? The author of Isaiah xl–lv had found the answer; not only was the 'Suffering Servant' to be the new pattern, but also it was to be a pattern not merely for the Jews but for the whole earth. There must be a new Covenant. So the temptation to 'restore the kingdom to Israel' was put aside.

Then how to convey His message? By performing miracles to force indifferent hearers to realise the nature of Himself and His mission? This, too, He realised, would be an abuse of His power. To use His exceptional powers for the relief of suffering and the overcoming of evil would be justified; and if those powers were an added proof of His authenticity to those who already had the spiritual insight to recognise Him, this too would be warranted. But to perform signs and wonders just to convince the incredulous would be to reveal a false picture of the Divine nature, quite apart from being no more permanently effective than the conjuring tricks of a mountebank. So it had to be the hard way, the way of the Suffering Servant, the path of preaching and teaching rather than the path of power.

This, then, is the first thread of the drama, one which needs to be appreciated by the teacher from the very beginning if its dramatic quality is to be utilised. It should be remembered that, although summarised at the beginning of His ministry, Jesus' temptations were recurrent from the days in the wilderness right up to the Cross. They protrude at various places in the narrative and at these points this thread of the drama should be made prominent before being once more woven back into the complete texture. As His gospel of the Kingdom failed to win general recognition, there was a progressive realisation that His path lay along the road to persecution. He gave more attention to the initiation of a select band into the real meaning of His mission. Yet even in this His disciples misunderstood Him; only where there was already a certain degree of spiritual insight could He be fully accepted.

The other two threads of the drama are connected. The first thread lies, as we have seen, in Jesus' own conception of His mission, His choice of the appropriate method to fulfil it, and His consistency in working it out. The second thread lies in the progressive realisation of His mission by others. Realisation was gradual, and had many setbacks; although it can be said that a climax is reached when Peter speaks for the Twelve at Caesarea Philippi, this thread of the drama is in some ways more prominent after the Resurrection, and runs right on into Acts.

The opposition Jesus aroused provides the third thread of the drama. On the one hand He quickly gained a certain fame and popularity with the common people; but on the other, this in itself roused the antagonism of the religious authorities, who failed to see His teaching as a fulfilment of the Law and the Prophets; they had a vested interest in the preservation of the Law as it stood, and regarded His teaching as subversive propaganda which canalised public discontent against them and which might prejudice their privileged position. This thread can continually be picked out from the fabric of the story, as popularity increased and opposition hardened, culminating in the Palm Sunday procession on the one side, and the Cross on the other.

The conspiracy against Jesus, His apparent defeat in the Crucifixion, followed by His final triumph in the Resurrection, naturally have prominence in the story. The second and third threads of the drama are continued into Acts, where the whole can be concluded with the final understanding of Jesus' Messiahship on the part of the apostles, together with the new-found courage with which they proclaimed it after the descent of the Holy Spirit. Although some of the Pharisees were won over, the antagonism of the Sadducees increased with the proclaiming of a resurrection. Thus there was continued opposition and jealousy from the religious authorities, although they themselves began to doubt the finality of their own victory. This is the point at which the drama of the Life of Christ can best be rounded off, for it is also here that another begins—that of the growth of the community of His followers and the spread of Christianity as a world religion.

THE LIFE OF CHRIST
(Based on St Mark's Gospel and Acts i–iv)

'Now we see glowing through the gospel pages the lines of the portrait of a real person, we are beginning to grasp the central fact of the Christian faith—the reality of Jesus.' (GEORGE B. JEFFERY.)

The Coming of the Christ (St Luke ii. 39–iii. 23; St Mark i. 1–11)

The boy in the temple; John the Baptist is shown to fulfil the prophecies of Malachi (Malachi iii. 1) and Isaiah (Isaiah xl. 3) in preparing people for Christ's coming; at His baptism Jesus is declared to be the beloved Son of God.

The Temptation (St Mark i. 12–13 and St Luke iv. 1–13)

Jesus suffers the same temptations as men and is particularly tempted concerning the aim of His mission and the means to be adopted in carrying it out.

The Galilean Ministry (St Mark i. 14–viii. 26). Preaching the Gospel of the Kingdom to the Crowds.

Jesus favourably received by the crowd (St Mark i. 14–35)

The proclamation of the Kingdom of God marks the beginning of Jesus' ministry; the first disciples are called; healing and preaching brings popularity.

A series of conflicts between Jesus and the Pharisees (St Mark ii. 1–22; St Luke vii. 19–35; xv. 3–32; St Mark ii. 23–iii. 6)

As the friend of publicans and sinners announcing that the joyful news of the Kingdom is not something which can just be tacked on to the kill-joy legalism of the Pharisees, and that it is more for the outcast than the self-righteous, Jesus comes into conflict with the Pharisees. What they regard as His sacrilegious attitude to the Sabbath intensifies their opposition, which increases right up to the climax of the drama and leads to their conspiring with the Herodians against His life.

Jesus meets the opposition (St Mark iii. 7–19)

He continues His work of healing, and appoints 'the twelve'.

Aggravation of the conflict (St Mark iii. 20–35)

Jesus' own kinsfolk think Him out of His mind, and the Pharisees say He is possessed by the devil.

A Specimen of the Teaching of Jesus (St Mark iv. 1–34)

The sower and 'seed' parables explain the nature of the Kingdom and describe different responses to it.

Jesus leaves Galilee for heathen territory (St Mark iv. 35–v. 43)

Though He is not ill-received, the time for work among non-Jews has not yet come.

Further opposition on His return to Galilee (St Mark vi. 1–30)

Jesus sends the Twelve out on a mission. The death of John the Baptist and Herod's anxiety about Jesus serve as a reminder of the seriousness of the opposition and its logical outcome.

One More Appeal to the Multitudes (St Mark vi. 31–vii. 23)

There seem to be two accounts of the feeding of the multitudes (St Mark vi. 30–44 and viii. 1–9; the parallelism in the consequences is striking), indicating the special importance attached to it in the Gospel tradition; the distribution of the loaves was conceived as an anticipation of the Lord's Supper.[1] The people do not wholeheartedly respond to Jesus' appeals to them, which provoke further opposition. The fate of Jesus' public ministry is now determined. He gives up teaching intended to win the multitudes.

The Instruction of the Disciples. The Messianic Secret
(St Mark vii. 24–ix. 50)

Jesus takes His disciples more or less into retirement, and for the most part on foreign soil to the north and north-east of Galilee. One purpose of this retirement is to avoid the hostility of Herod and of the religious authorities with whom He is not prepared to join decisive issue until He has completed the other purpose of this retirement—a more intensive concentration of His work upon the inner company of disciples. In this section of the narrative, the importance of the incidents in which other people appear, such as the story of the Rich Young Ruler, is in the special teaching for the disciples which is attached to them. Corresponding to the

---

[1] For a more detailed treatment of this idea, see p. 150.

change in those addressed is a change in the character of the instruction: it is no longer a Gospel of the Kingdom, but the Gospel of the Messiah. Peter's confession has a place of quite special importance in this part of the gospel; it is the turning-point of the drama. Thereafter the Messiahship of Jesus is central both in the narrative and in the instruction given to the disciples. Jesus reveals to them what will be the outcome of His conflict with the religious authorities and His fate at Jerusalem. Through the Transfiguration a deeper realisation is given to a chosen few; He foretells His suffering and resurrection, but they fail to understand. After each prediction of the sufferings and resurrection of the Messiah, Mark puts an episode which emphasises the disciples' lack of comprehension—the Epileptic Boy, the Dispute about Precedence, and, later, the request of the sons of Zebedee.

The Last Journey (St Mark x and St Luke ix. 51–62)

Jesus comes into the open again, as He resolutely leaves Galilee for the South. Now that the disciples have some understanding of the Messianic secret, He is ready for the conflict with the religious authorities which an open declaration of His message will make inevitable. The blind beggar's acclamation of Him as 'Son of David' (a Jewish title for the Messiah) is given as a recognition of Jesus' Messiahship outside the circle of the disciples.

Jesus' Challenge to Jerusalem
(St Mark xi, xii; St John vii. 14–53)

At the height of His popularity Jesus enters Jerusalem in a manner suggesting the Messiah as described in Zechariah ix. 9. The cleansing of the Temple makes Jesus' claim and position clear. Discussions with the Jews accentuate and define the conflict, but His answers to a series of catch-questions fail to give the religious authorities any legal grounds for accusing Him. Jesus' outspoken denunciation of them makes them determined to silence Him; His popularity precludes open arrest, so they resort to conspiracy.

Christ's Suffering (St Mark xiv; xv)

The story of the Passion, as told by St Mark, forms a closely connected narrative. We see the final conspiracy taking shape, and the opposing forces apparently win.

Christ's Victory (St Mark xvi. 1–8; I Corinthians xv. 3–8;
St Mark xvi. 9–20; Acts i. 1–14)

Though the forces of evil have seemed to triumph, the real victory is with Christ, who convinces His disciples that He is not dead but alive, and is now set free from the necessary limitations of His life on earth.

Some women followers of Jesus go on the Sunday after the Crucifixion to anoint their Master's body in the tomb. There they see a young man who tells them that He whom they seek is no longer there, He is risen. But in their amazement and fear the women tell no one of this experience.

At this point (xvi. 8) St Mark's Gospel breaks off; whether the evangelist intended to end here, or his original ending was somehow accidentally lost, we cannot tell. What follows (*vv.* 9–20) is a brief summary, added later, of the accounts given in the other three Gospels of the appearances of the risen Christ to His disciples. It is not easy to harmonise these accounts either with one another or with the earliest list of the appearances, that given by St Paul in I Corinthians xv.

But there is no doubt about the effect of their experiences upon the disciples; they are convinced that Jesus has triumphed over death and His enemies, and won salvation for those who believe on Him; and that they are commissioned and empowered to be effective witnesses for Him. According to Acts i. 1–14, the risen Christ continues to be with them in this way for forty days, and during this time they come to understand that He is not an earthly Messiah who should 'restore the Kingdom to Israel', but the heavenly Lord 'at the right hand of God'. His exaltation is pictorially represented in the story of His 'Ascension'.

The Beginnings of the Church (Acts i. 15–iv. 37)

The natural leaders of the first small group of believers are the apostles whom Jesus Himself had chosen. The gap in their company made by the defection and death of Judas is repaired by the election of Matthias in his stead. The descent of the Spirit at Pentecost marks the beginning of the new order, in which the community is given guidance and power by the Holy Spirit. Peter is the spokesman, and proclaims that what has happened is the fulfilment of the promises of God made through the Old Testament prophets. The fellowship created by the Spirit is manifested in the common worship, in 'the breaking of bread' (the early form of the Lord's Supper), and in the sharing of possessions. The Church continues the preaching and healing work of Jesus, and the attempts of the Jewish authorities to hinder it are ineffective in face of the manifest power of the Spirit.

II. Outstanding Events in Old Testament History

Many religious difficulties are created because of a misunderstanding of the nature and composite character of the Old Testament writings. It is only by realising the various points of view from which the different Old Testament authors write, and by regarding the Old Testament as history seen in the light of the purpose of God, that these difficulties will be solved. The Old Testament should not be approached primarily as a piece of great literature, or as a scientific text-book, or even as a manual for devotional use, but as the record (of necessity rough, imperfect and even touched with prejudice, because expressed through a human medium) of the experience of God of a particular people, in whose history the prophetic eye can see the working out of the divine purpose.

It is easy for Old Testament background teaching to seem irrelevant to children who are past the 'story' stage. It will be a help to minimise this tendency if the teacher keeps in mind not merely the immediate study but its relation to the work of coming years, for which a certain knowledge and understanding are necessary. It is important for children at this stage to gain an outline knowledge of Old Testament history, right up to the time of Christ, so that Jesus can be seen as coming into a real world with its own problems; so that current ideas underlying His teaching (such as those of the Messiah, the Kingdom, the Law), may be understood in their context; and so that the picture can be shown of a people who recognise God as active in their history and as working out His plans for men.

Teachers who do not take the older age-groups should therefore make a point of seeing their own work in relation to the whole course and to later needs. This does not invite any forcing of children to conceptions beyond their years but should result in the kind of selection and treatment of subject-matter that awakens growing interest and provides the factual background necessary for later reference. The adult, whilst he will find his conviction through the Christ of experience, will deepen it, clarify it and justify it through the Jesus of history; the years from 11 onwards have a particular contribution to make towards this confirmation.

It is suggested that the normal methods of teaching history, such as time-charts and projects, may well be employed in the scripture lesson. A class could usefully build up a diagrammatic outline, with illustrations and Biblical references, which could be used for later revision and expansion. Learning by heart, if not forced or made deadly by dreary repetition, makes an invaluable contribution. (The teacher is recommended to read carefully the section on this subject on pp. 141–143.) Passages chosen should be those which reveal understanding about God, His relationships with men, passages referred to in the Gospels, or those relevant to central conceptions, such as the moral law, the Covenant and the hope of Israel.

The Promise of the Fathers

The stories of the Patriarchs in the form in which we have them, were written down at a time much later than that to which they refer. They were derived from a much larger mass of material, written and oral, and were adapted for a definite purpose. They explain the position of the Israelites as a 'peculiar people'. The stress falls on the Promise made by God successively to the three patriarchs Abraham, Isaac and Jacob. In broadest outline, in which there is no clear distinction between legend, folklore and history, we see the beginnings of God's choice of his people Israel which is the starting-point of all Jewish and Christian history. The background of these stories agrees with the picture which archaeologists have reconstructed from their findings of this early period.

> Abraham (Genesis xi. 27–xxv. 18). The promise is frequently made (xii. 2; xiii. 14–17; xv. 13–16; xvii. 4; and again in xxii. 17 after Abraham's obedience has been tested; his faith makes him willing to sacrifice Isaac, but he is shown that God does not demand human sacrifice).

Isaac (Genesis xxi. 1–5; xxii; xxiv; xxv. 19–xxviii. 9). The promise is repeated (xxv. 21–23; xxvi. 3–5, 24).

Jacob (Genesis xxv. 24–34; xxviii. 1–5, 10–22). The promise is made many times and passed on to Jacob's children (Genesis xxviii. 13–15; xxv. 11–12); the story of Jacob's dream shows God thought of as specially present in certain places.

Joseph and his brethren (Genesis xxxvii; xlii; xlv). The descent into Egypt (Genesis xlvi–xlvii. 12).

The Exodus

The later Jews always looked back to the Exodus for the assurance of God's guidance and the working out of His purpose in the events of human history. It must not be forgotten that this was the point of view from which the stories were written.

God is shown as choosing a people, delivering them, and revealing Himself to them (Exodus iii, vi; xix). Moses is the outstanding figure (Exodus i–xviii; xxiv; xxxii; Numbers xi–xiii; xvi; Deuteronomy i–iii; xxxi–xxxiv). His importance lies in the part he played in the establishment among the Israelites of the worship of the God whose name was 'Yahweh' (Jehovah), and the binding of Israel to this God in a formal covenant, 'I will be your God, and ye shall be my people' (Jeremiah vii. 22–23; Exodus xxiv). Recognising Yahweh as the divine champion who had brought them out of Egypt, the Israelites bound themselves to observe a certain way of life and conduct, summarised in the Ten Commandments (Deuteronomy v). The Israelites entered Palestine in fulfilment of Yahweh's promises (Joshua i–vi).

The Monarchy

After the settlement in Palestine (told in different accounts in Joshua and Judges) the leaders were 'Judges' given by God for special needs. Attempts are made to found a kingship (Judges viii. 22–23; I Samuel viii). The two stories of the institution of the monarchy clearly show two points of view: (i) I Samuel viii; x. 17–24; xii. (ii) I Samuel ix–x. 16; xi. 1–11. With Samuel we have the real beginning of that great line of prophets whose business it was to recall the nation again and again to its true religion and purpose. Samuel had a vision of the glorious rule of God; in Saul and the monarchy he hoped that this Kingdom of God would be established in the face of Philistine opposition (I Samuel ix. 15–17). But his expectations were disappointed on account of human failings, and his vision only found its true fulfilment in the Gospel of the New Testament.

The chief centre of interest in the monarchy is David, to whom God's promise is made (II Samuel vii). Many stories illustrate God's choice of him (I Samuel xvi); his prowess (xvii); his friendship with Jonathan (xviii–xx); the growth of his kingdom, over Judah (II Samuel ii), over Israel and the Philistines (II Samuel v), over Syria (II Samuel viii), over Ammon (II Samuel x). The reigns of David and Solomon are later idealised as the Golden Age, but no human king is good enough to rule God's people; David and his successors sin and fail, making way for the hope of God's Anointed Messiah sitting on David's throne. David's great sin with Bathsheba (II Samuel xi–xii. 25) is told as leading to Absalom's revolt (II Samuel xiv–xviii) and the revolt in the North.

In the reign of Solomon (I Kings i–xi) the Temple is built (I Kings iii. 1–4; vi. 1–9; viii. 1–21), but his sin, of compromising with paganism, is seen as causing the revolt of Edom, Syria and the North (I Kings xi).

The Division of the Kingdom

North and South Palestine are geographically distinct; their people came from different areas, and their religious symbols were not the same. David and Solomon united the two by arms, but Solomon's extravagance caused a revolt at the end of his reign. The southern historians condemned all northern kings as schismatics, and interest in the North centres round Elijah and Elisha.

The Disruption (I Kings xi. 26–40; xii).

Elijah's contest with the prophets of Baal as to who is the true God (I Kings xvii–xix; II Kings i) serves to characterise the nature of the religious struggle of the time.

The effects of prophetic religion show themselves in Elijah's denunciation of Ahab in connection with Naboth's vineyard (I Kings xxi); God demands right conduct.

The Warnings of the Prophets

The Prophets saw the threat of invasion, interpreted the history of their day as God's designs to punish the nation's sins, and called the nation to repentance.

Amos. His interpretation of recent events (iv. 6–12), and his pictures of the state of the nation (vii–viii).

Hosea, whose love for a faithless wife was the parable of God's love for a faithless people (i–iii).

Isaiah. His call (vi); the messages to Ahaz (vii) and to Hezekiah (xxxvi–xxxvii).

The Fall of the Kingdoms

The North fell to Assyria in 721 B.C.; the southern writer tells of its sins (II Kings xvii) and of the escape of the South (I Kings xix). The South fell to Babylon in 586 B.C. (II Kings xxiii. 36–xxv). Jeremiah is the outstanding figure, called to deliver an unpopular message (Jeremiah i) and doing so in spite of persecution (Jeremiah xxiv; xxvi; xxxviii).

The new governor, Gedaliah, was murdered (Jeremiah xl–xli. 2).

The Exile

Ezekiel. One of the exiles; his call (i. 1–3); his message through the death of his wife (xxiv. 15–24); his discovery that God was with the exiles in Babylonia and that men are not helplessly bound by their past if they now turn to God (xviii; xxxiii. 1–20); the exiles' attitude towards him (xxxiii. 21–33).

The author of Isaiah xl–lv (sometimes called 'The Unknown Prophet', or 'Second Isaiah'). A message of comfort (xl); Cyrus greeted as a Saviour (xlv. 1–7).

The first return takes place about 536 B.C. (Ezra i).

Reconstruction in Palestine

Haggai urges the rebuilding of the Temple (Haggai i–ii. 9); Zechariah's objection to rebuilding the walls (Zechariah ii); Nehemiah's return in 444 B.C. and the rebuilding of the walls (Nehemiah i; ii; iv; vi; xii. 27); his second visit in 432 B.C. (Nehemiah xiii. 4–31); Ezra's return about 397 B.C. (Ezra vii–viii); reading the Law-book (Nehemiah viii). (The above dates are probable, not certain.)

The Maccabean Revolt

After 333 B.C. Palestine became part of the Greek empire of Alexander the Great. Following the division of his kingdom at his death there was rivalry between the Seleucid kings of Syria to the north of Palestine and the Ptolemies in Egypt. Eventually the Seleucids gained control of Palestine, but in 167 B.C. a great revolt broke out against the then ruling king of Syria, Antiochus IV.

The beginning of the revolt (I Maccabees ii. 1–48); Judas (I Maccabees iii. 1–9); his successes and failures (I Maccabees iii. 10–iv); alliance with Rome (I Maccabees viii); death of Judas (I Maccabees ix); wise reign of Simon the Priest-King (I Maccabees xiv. 25–49); John Hyrcanus embarks on a policy of aggrandisement, which was continued by Alexander Jannaeus and led to civil war; one party seeks Roman 'protection', and in 63 B.C. an army under Pompey captures Jerusalem with the assistance of Antipater, whose son Herod is confirmed as King of the Jews by the Romans.

CHILDREN AGED 13–15

I. THE GOSPEL OF JESUS CHRIST

Jesus was born among a people who were convinced that they held a specially privileged position among the nations of the world in their possession of true knowledge of God. For the Jews it was this special relationship with God which had preserved them in all the fluctuating fortunes of a small nation surrounded by large and powerful neighbours. For two generations before the birth of Jesus civil war and foreign domination had followed the brief period of independence under the Maccabees. The Jews were therefore expectant, looking for a deliverer sent by God Himself. 'All men mused in their hearts of John, whether he were the Christ or not'; 'Art thou he that should come, or do we look for another?' God was not thought of merely as a first cause, or as a principle of righteousness, but as the living God active in human history. When faced by the problem of sin and evil they were forced to postulate a Day of the Lord when the power of evil would be vanquished and the perfect rule of God would come. This Kingdom of God was never envisaged as the natural culmination of history, but as brought about by an act of God.

It was this great religious tradition which Jesus inherited and used creatively. There had been hints in earlier Jewish thought that the Jews had not been chosen for their own sake only (Jeremiah, Isaiah xl–lv, the Books of Ruth and Jonah); it was these suggestions particularly which Jesus developed further. He did not merely fulfil a national hope; He brought a message of God which was for the whole world.

In studying the Gospels this twofold development should be borne in mind. There is the tracing of the Gospel story as the fulfilment of the Jewish hope, which is the main concern of St Matthew's Gospel, and the recognition of the universal character of the Christian message, which St Luke links up with the world situation. The Prologue of St John reinterprets this Gospel again in terms of current philosophical thought.

In considering this world-wide nature of Jesus' teaching care should be taken to show that it is universal in time as well as in space, and that its principles, necessarily enunciated by Jesus in the idiom of His own day or by concrete example in the circumstances of His time, still apply to-day even if social and economic conditions have changed. The modern application of the teaching of Jesus has always tended to be a controversial matter, but teachers should not avoid dealing with it for that reason. This is the occasion to present as clear and positive an account of Jesus' teaching as possible. The presentation need not always be direct; at this stage children should be encouraged to discuss, to debate, to make their own discoveries from 'original sources'. More and more should the expression of individual thought and the voicing of individual difficulties be encouraged. Perhaps the relevance of Christian teaching to modern times can most effectively be illustrated from the lives of men and women with the courage and honesty to apply Christ's teaching fearlessly to the circumstances of their time. Reference should be made to some of those mentioned on pp. 81–82, and teachers should try to find as much illustrative material as possible from situations with which their pupils are acquainted.

In connection with this section the teacher is recommended to study carefully the note on 'Miracles in the New Testament' on p. 148. It will be sufficient here to emphasise that the miracles of the Gospel are not to be viewed as isolated works of wonder, indisputable proofs of divinity or arbitrary interferences in the natural order; rather they are the incidental indications of divine power breaking into human life in the person of Jesus. The Divine has never been manifested on earth to the same extent before or since; it is to be expected that such a manifestation will be accompanied by happenings outside the usual range of human experience. These acts arose out of circumstances and represent the divine response to human need.

The Birth of Jesus Christ

St Mark (i. 1) envisaged the coming of Jesus as an act of God, and the same underlying mystery is expressed in the birth stories of St Matthew and St Luke.

> The fulfilment of the prophetic hope of the nation (St Matthew i. 18–24; ii. 13–23; St Luke i. 26–55; ii. 8–20, 22–39).
> The Saviour of the world (St Luke ii. 1–20; St Matthew ii. 1–12).

The stories will already be familiar; it will now be possible to show their symbolic significance—the shepherds and the wise men representing Jew and Gentile, poor and rich, simple and wise; Jesus came to be the Saviour of all.

The Mission of Jesus Christ

Baptism

Jesus dedicates himself to the will of the Father and receives an inward assurance of God's approval and choice of Him for some special work (St Matthew iii).

Temptation

Jesus has now to decide just what His work is to be and how He is to fulfil it. In making these decisions He faces temptations to make his appeal by promises of material prosperity, by means of sensational and spectacular achievements or by pursuing worldly ends instead of preaching a spiritual kingdom. Jesus rejects these temptations with words taken from the Scriptures and provides the answers to the ever-present temptations to try to bring in the Kingdom by feeding men's bodies, by coercing their minds or by trying to attain good ends by evil means. Jesus affirms His faith in God, by whose action alone the Kingdom of God is brought about (St Matthew iv. 1-11) and in St Luke iv. 1-21 we have a programme of the positive course He is to follow in contrast to those means He has rejected.

The Teaching of Jesus

Our Father...

For Jesus and His hearers the reality of God is never in question: the world is God's creation in which God is constantly at work. Jesus speaks of 'the Kingdom of God', but He usually calls God not 'King' but 'Father'—one who, though not indulgent in the bad sense, is generous to the undeserving (St Matthew v. 45-48; St Luke xv. 11-32), and intensely concerned about every person, animal and blade of grass (St Matthew vi. 25-34).

Like Father, like son (St Matthew v. 45-48)

We enter the Kingdom, become part of the family, by a change of attitude to the Father, by accepting His Fatherhood. This involves repentance and willingness to forgive others (St Mark i. 15; St Matthew xviii. 21-35), undivided loyalty (St Matthew vi. 24; St Mark x. 17-31), obedience to God's call through the needs of others (St Matthew xxv. 31-46; St Luke x. 25-37), avoiding unkind criticism (St Matthew vii. 1-6), fortitude and perseverance (St Luke ix. 62; xxi. 19), a right motive and an inward attitude (St Matthew v. 1-12, 21-24, 27-32; vi. 1-15), vigilance (St Matthew xxv. 1-13; St Luke xii. 35-38), and absolute confidence in God (St Mark xi. 22-24).

Thy Kingdom Come...

The Kingdom already exists ('as it is in heaven'); God is in complete control.

But it also 'comes' with the coming of Jesus (St Luke vii. 22; x. 11; xi. 20); Jesus as the Christ (that is 'Messiah', or God's Anointed King) represents the Kingdom; as the Son of God, He sums up the perfect and unspoilt family life.

Moreover, the Kingdom 'comes' whenever an individual is willing to be ruled by God, and so to become a subject of the

Kingdom (St Mark xii. 34; St Luke xvii. 21; St John iv. 23, 24; v. 24).

Yet a future, universal manifestation is also assumed in the teaching of the Gospels, when the good and the bad shall be distinguished (St Matthew xiii. 24–30, 36–43, 47–50; xxv. 14–46).

The Passion and Resurrection

Peter's confession of faith (St Mark viii. 27–ix. 1) in Jesus as the Messiah gives Him the opportunity of presenting His own conception of Messiahship pictured in Isaiah liii (St Matthew xvi. 21–28; xx. 28; St John xv). It is not suggested that the writer of Isaiah liii pointed to Jesus of Nazareth, but that Jesus found in the writer's conception of the Suffering Servant a new possibility of Messiahship through a life of redemptive suffering. Realising that the fate of His mission cannot be decided outside Jerusalem, He 'sets his face' to go thither (St Luke ix. 51–56).

The trend of events leads to the Cross. The crowds are disappointed at His refusal to accept an earthly kingship (St John vi. 15), the Pharisees are antagonised by His attacks on their narrow nationalism (St Luke iv. 24–28), the Sadducees by His teaching about the resurrection (St Matthew xxii. 23–33) and by His attitude to the temple (St Luke xix. 45–46; St Matthew xxvi. 61), and the Herodians by His criticism of Herod (St Luke xiii. 31–33). The religious authorities conspire against Him (St John xi. 47–53) while the crowds acclaim Him (St John xii. 12–19) and some non-Jews are interested (St John xii. 20–22). The claim to a kingship and the fear of an insurrection implicates the Roman Governor (St John xviii. 33–40; xix. 12–16).

The Crucifixion

The penitent thief (St Luke xxiii. 34–43), the reference to Psalm xxii (St Matthew xxvii. 46), the cry of victory (St John xix. 30), the recognition of the centurion (St Mark xv. 39).

The Resurrection

The empty tomb (St Matthew xxviii. 1–15), on the road to Emmaus (St Luke xxiv. 13–35), the appearance to the disciples and to Thomas (St John xx. 19–29), the universal charge (St Matthew xxviii. 16–20).

The Spread of the Gospel

Christ's Ascension

This, it seems, was God's way of impressing on the friends of Jesus that the period when they could *see* Him present was terminated, and the era of His unseen, unrestricted presence was about to open. It must have been an important prelude to Pentecost to learn confidence in His constant companionship without the limited evidence of sight. At the Ascension Christ's person—hitherto associated by His friends with the visible shape, limited in time and space—is 'let loose in all the world'.

That the upward movement should symbolise this is easier to understand when one remembers that, in the Bible, heaven, the dwelling-place of God and His angels, is thought of as spatially located above the earth and sky, just as Sheol or Hades, the abode of the spirits of the dead, is thought of as located below the earth. Even when it was realised that God's presence was not confined to heaven (Psalm cxxxix. 8) it was still natural to speak of going to where God 'dwelt' as 'ascending' (Acts i. 6-14).

Pentecost

After the day of Pentecost the disciples embarked upon a course of action of which there had been no suggestion among the confused and dispirited followers of Jesus after the Crucifixion (St Luke xxiv. 21; St John xx. 19). How did this come about? The answer is that a profound change had been wrought in them; they were transformed by their conviction of the Resurrection and by the advent of the Holy Spirit. The disciples then knew that, just as they had been taught and guided by Jesus before, so they were now taught and guided in a common purpose by the Spirit. Their experience is naturally described in the imagery of Jewish symbolism; at Pentecost the Jews celebrated the giving of the Law on Sinai with all the phenomena of wind and fire (Exodus xix. 16-19) representing the power and person of God. (This symbolism can also be seen in I Kings xix. 11-13, where surprise is expressed that God was *not* in the wind or fire. To show that they were not imprisoned by their own metaphors, notice Peter's claim in Acts ii. 16-21 that the prophecies of Joel ii. 28-32 concerning celestial phenomena had that day been fulfilled in

Jerusalem, although it was not suggested that any actual disturbance had occurred in the heavens.) Among the Jews of the time of Christ wine had become a symbol of the Law-giving, and although Peter denies that the disciples were drunk, the early Christians realised at Pentecost that the 'new wine' of the Gospel and the Spirit had burst the 'old wineskins' of the Law (Acts ii. 1–42).

Stephen: the Parting of the Ways

The main body of early Christians observe the Jewish Law and are held in favour of all the people; but the Greek-speaking Christians in the Early Church seem to have taken a larger view of the Gospel (Acts vi. 2–8). Among them, Stephen is the leading figure. As the forerunner of Paul in his concept of the universality of the Gospel, he is accused of subverting the religion of Israel and is brought before the Sanhedrin (Acts vi. 9–15). He defends himself by quoting Isaiah to show that God is not confined to 'temples made with hands', and by demonstrating, from a review of traditional Jewish history, that Jesus was the fulfilment of God's purpose for mankind, but that, just as the prophets were persecuted, so His contemporaries had killed the Christ instead of recognising and accepting Him (Acts vii. 1–4, 29–36, 44–53). The result is that an angry mob stones Stephen, and Paul 'consents' (Acts vii. 54–viii. 3). General persecution ensues, and the Gospel is spread to Samaria and beyond (Acts viii. 4–40). With hesitation Peter obeys the vision to take the Gospel to Gentiles (Acts x–xi. 18).

The Preaching to the Gentiles

Paul the Persecutor

A Jew of Tarsus, a Pharisee, a pupil of Gamaliel, a Roman citizen, a persecutor of the early Christians (Acts viii. 1, 3; xxi. 39; xxii. 3–5; Philippians iii. 3–6).

His mission to Damascus, conversion and baptism (Acts ix. 1–22), sojourn in Arabia (Galatians, i. 15–17), return to Damascus and Jerusalem, and journey to Tarsus (Acts ix. 23–31).

Paul the Christian

Brought from Tarsus to Antioch by Barnabas (Acts xi. 19–30); journey to Cyprus, Pisidian Antioch ('Lo, we turn to the Gentiles') and cities of Galatia (Acts xiii–xiv). It is possible that it was just after this journey that Paul wrote his letter to the Galatians (Galatians i–ii; iii. 23–29; vi. 14–18).

The Universal Gospel

At the Council of Jerusalem it is decided that Gentiles may be admitted into the Church (Acts xv. 1–35).

Paul undertakes his second missionary journey; he preaches at Philippi, Thessalonica and Athens, and comes to Corinth (Acts xv. 36–xviii. 18); he stays there two years and writes to one of the churches recently founded (I Thessalonians i. 1–7; II Thessalonians iii. 6–18).

Work at Ephesus (Acts xviii. 19–xix) and letters to Christians in Corinth (I Corinthians i. 1–25; ix. 24–27; xi. 17–29; xii. 1–13; xiii; xv. 1–20, 35–38, 54–55; II Corinthians x. 17–18; xi. 3–5, 16–18, 22–23). Paul revisits Greece (Acts xx. 1–3), writes to Christians in Rome (Romans i. 1–12; viii. 35–39; xi. 1–5; xii; xv. 13, 24–33), and returns to Jerusalem (Acts xx. 4–xxi. 26).

From Jerusalem to Rome

Paul's arrest and his trials before the Sanhedrin and at Caesarea (Acts xxi. 27–xxiv).

It is possible that Paul had already planned to visit Rome in order to carry out missionary work in the west (Romans xv. 24), and his appeal from the local authorities to the emperor (Acts xxv–xxvi) results in his travelling thither as a prisoner (Acts xxvii–xxviii. 16).

At Rome (Acts xxviii. 17–31) he writes to the Philippians (Philippians i. 1–14; iv. 4–8), the Colossians (Colossians i. 1–2; iv. 1–9, 14–18), the Ephesians (Ephesians i. 1–3; ii. 13–22; iv. 1–7; vi. 10–24) and to Philemon (Philemon).

Thus the universal gospel of Jesus Christ, springing out of the national hopes of Israel, reaches the heart of the Roman Empire.

II. THE DEVELOPMENT OF IDEAS ABOUT BEHAVIOUR, MAN AND GOD IN THE OLD TESTAMENT

The knowledge of the Old Testament gained in the preceding years should be used as a framework into which can be fitted the development of those important aspects which previously the children were not ready to study.

The primary requirement is to get a right approach to the question of prophecy, rendered harder by the modern cheapening of the word. A 'prophet' in the Old Testament was one who spoke to men on behalf of God. It was only through the obedient response of these humble men of heart that Israel was again and again recalled to its true vocation. The prophets pondered over the affairs of the nation, communed with God, and, blessed with greater spiritual insight than their fellows, delivered His messages to the people. They were not primarily concerned with forecasting future events, 'the prophetic soul of the wide world dreaming on things to come', but with the interpretation of the present and the proclamation of God's will for it. By the prophets, God was thought of as the Living God active in human history. This theme runs throughout the Old Testament, but the divine action and purpose were continually misunderstood and rebelled against; actions were ascribed to God which, in the light of the knowledge of Him revealed in Christ, can no longer be regarded as worthy of Him.

It is necessary to realise that the religious experience of the prophets did not differ essentially from that of religious people of to-day. Those reading the prophetic writings are sometimes misled by the manner in which religious convictions are expressed in much more vivid and concrete language than we are nowadays accustomed to use when speaking of such experiences. This may suggest that God 'spoke' to the prophets in a way altogether different from that in which He now speaks to those who will listen. 'Thus saith the Lord' is a common formula which may refer to an abnormal sense of hearing God's voice (compare the account in I Samuel iii); or, perhaps more often, simply to an intuitive conviction that what follows expresses God's will. Similarly, 'The Lord God shewed me...' (Amos viii. 1) or 'I saw the Lord...' (Amos ix. 1; compare Isaiah vi. 1) may refer to abnormal, ecstatic 'vision', or to what we should simply call a 'vivid' experience. But what really matters is not how God spoke to the prophets, and through them to His people Israel, but that God did speak to and through men. The positive conclusion is the underlying sense of being in touch with God.

At this age, children are often deeply interested in moral and social problems of the kind which present themselves in their own experience. The writers of the Old Testament, especially the prophets, are very largely concerned with problems of this kind. If the children are brought to understand this, and how men need to study 'their times' and their duty in relation to God, their study of the Bible will serve an immediate practical purpose. The prophets had a true picture of their times, by being drawn to seek for God and to 'meet with' Him. Not only did they learn new truths about Him, but they were able to see the world anew, from His angle as it were, and so to recognise its real needs. This enabled them to proclaim His 'word'—His message both of condemnation and of hope. Gradually there is built up through the Old Testament this picture of great persons pointing towards a greater to come.

It will be well to keep in mind the close relation between the Old and the New Testaments, and to remember that the Old Testament, with its vivid and concrete method of expressing ideas, was a part of the living religious tradition inherited and used creatively by Jesus, to which the New Testament writers are continually referring. Jesus Himself must have pondered for years upon the real significance of the Old Testament before embarking upon His ministry.

> 'So all their praises are but prophecies
> Of this our time, all you prefiguring.'

In tracing the development of the religious ideas of the Old Testament the main purpose in the mind of the teacher should be to show their relationship to the New Testament; to make clear that without the contribution which the Hebrews made to religious thought and life, Jesus would not have been able to make His teaching understood. 'Think not that I am come to destroy, but to fulfil.' It is possible to demonstrate a number of successive stages in the principal Old Testament ideas and beliefs concerning Behaviour, Man and God, which all lead up to the supreme revelation in Jesus Christ.

Kings and Prophets in Israel

At the beginning of the monarchy sin is thought of as something that 'is not done in Israel' (I Samuel xiii. 5–14; xxv. 1–39), or as an unwitting breach of a taboo (I Samuel xv, where the ruthless destruction of Israel's pagan enemies is regarded as necessary at that stage; I Samuel xxvi. 5–12); sin brings punishment not only on the sinner (I Samuel xv. 26) but also upon the whole community (Exodus xx. 5); ideas about the after-life are seen in I Samuel xv. 29; xxviii. 1–20.

The prophets of Israel appear to have been responsible for the marriage of morals and religion in Palestine. Earlier religion was more concerned with ritual acts and pilgrimages; the prophets taught that right conduct was the concern of God. The prophetic movement arose out of cruder beginnings; those believed to possess 'second sight' were consulted as seers (I Samuel ix. 1–20); Samuel seems to have lived when a change was coming about, and when the seer was giving place to the ecstatic prophet who gave forth utterances interpreted as divine messages (I Samuel x. 1–13). Nathan shows a higher form of prophecy by insisting, even to the king, that God demands right conduct (II Samuel xi–xii).

The children of Israel, in colonising the land of Canaan, changed from a nomadic, pastoral people into a settled agricultural community. The remnants of the Canaanites whom they had conquered were still living in the land, and it was from them that the newcomers learnt how to grow corn and olives and grapes. But for the Canaanites it was an essential part of their agricultural practice to gain the favour of the god of the land cultivated, in order that he might send rain and make the crops fertile; such local agricultural gods were called 'Baalim'. Their worship was accompanied by that of the Ashtaroth, or female goddesses of fecundity, whose favour was induced in a form of imitative magic. In teaching the Israelites the art of agriculture it was natural that the Canaanites should also teach them those practices which, to them, were essential to successful farming. The Israelites were no theologians; they saw no harm in old customs and ceremonies; so their devotion to Yahweh (Jehovah) became mingled with the worship of Baalim. Elijah convinces the Israelites that Yahweh is their true God (I Kings xviii); he sees another aspect of His character (I Kings xix); like Nathan before him, he insists that God demands right conduct and he is not afraid to show a king his fault; the story reinforces that of David and Bathsheba, illustrating how disobedience to the command not to covet (which means 'taking steps to obtain') leads to murder and adultery (I Kings xxi).

Jehu is consecrated by Elisha to continue Elijah's work of purifying the Israelites' worship of Yahweh from the contamination of Baal worship. The writer regards Jehu's ruthlessness in carrying this out as still necessary and as pleasing to God (II Kings ix; x).

The story of Naaman the Syrian (II Kings v) shows that Yahweh was thought of at this time as resident only in Palestine (*v.* 17).

The Eighth-Century Prophets

As the Israelites continually stray from the worship of Yahweh and from right conduct, so arise prophets to recall the nation to its true path, and to give loftier conceptions of God, with warnings of judgment and exile if the message is unheeded. Israel has sinned and forgotten God, and sin, whether in the individual or in the nation, ultimately involves suffering. Current political events are interpreted by the prophets in the light of the working out of God's purpose for Israel. Therefore He will use the growing menace of Assyria to punish; Assyria becomes the instrument of judgment. Yet, along with the message of judgment and the demand for social righteousness and justice, there is a promise of forgiveness if Israel will repent.

Amos makes no claim to be a professional prophet (Amos i. 1; vii. 14–15) but is filled with righteous indignation at the oppression of the poor, the injustice, and the senseless luxury which he sees, abuses which have grown up in a period of material prosperity; God is just and disaster will come if these things continue (Amos ii. 4–8; iii. 1–iv. 5; v. 10–15; vi; vii. 7–17; viii), nor can God be bribed by sacrifice and ceremony (Amos v. 21–27); God is seen as more than a mere tribal deity (Amos ix. 1–8).

Hosea declares that God not only rules but loves Israel like a husband or a father (Hosea xi. 1–4) and will do so even after transgression if the nation is repentant (Hosea ii. 19–iii. 5); as it is, the priests are as much to blame as the people (Hosea iv. 1–11); dependence on foreign nations is dangerous (vii. 8–16; viii. 8–10) because worship must not be contaminated with heathen practice (Hosea iv. 12–14; viii. 11–14), but in any case a right attitude is more important than ritual (Hosea vi. 4–11).

Micah feels that the professional prophets are misleading the people into complacency (Micah iii. 5–8); he stresses the sin of land-grabbing, and greed in all classes (Micah ii. 1–3, 8–11), pointing out that taking away a man's livelihood is equivalent to cannibalism (Micah iii. 1–4); he repeats the emphasis on right conduct (Micah vi. 6–9) and laments the scarcity of good men (Micah vii. 1–7).

Isaiah repeats the emphasis on right conduct (Isaiah i; x. 1–2); sin becomes an act against God, preventing men knowing Him (that is, having fellowship with Him; Isaiah ii. 3–4; compare Psalm li); particularly stressed are the evils of vanity (Isaiah ii. 5–22; iii. 16–24), drunkenness (Isaiah v. 11–13, 18–24) and reliance on diplomacy rather than on God (Isaiah xxxi); in a vision of the majesty of God, in which His righteousness is contrasted with man's imperfections, Isaiah lays a new emphasis on the holiness of God (Isaiah vi. 1–8) and in his interpretation of current affairs demands complete trust in God (Isaiah vii. 1–9; x. 5–23; xxx. 15).

Assyria destroys the Northern Kingdom (II Kings xvii. 9–20; xix).

Disregard and persecution of the prophets under Manasseh (II Kings xxi. 1–6, 16) is followed by the 'discovery' of the 'Book of the Law' (possibly the book of Deuteronomy) and the reforms of Josiah, by which religious observance is centralised and supervised in Jerusalem (II Kings xii; xxiii. 1–8).

The Captivity

In spite of the reforms of Josiah things go from bad to worse. Jeremiah is the outstanding figure, and with the fate of the Northern Kingdom before his eyes he becomes convinced of impending doom. The exile has become inevitable; Jerusalem will be taken and all her attempts at worldly power swept away. By their behaviour the Israelites have broken the Covenant and forfeited their right to divine protection. Yet for the prophet this is not the end, but a new beginning. Political independence may be lost, but through this very material loss of prosperity, men will be brought to a more spiritual understanding of God. There will be a new Covenant between God and His people, in which every member of the nation will know God's Law.

Jeremiah is reluctant to deliver his unpopular message (Jeremiah i. 4-8); he condemns survivals of animism (ii. 10-13, 26-28) and injustice (v. 25-30), and links right conduct with right worship (vii. 1-15, 21-24); his predictions of imminent disaster bring persecution (xxxvi. 9-32; xxxviii. 1-13); the new Covenant depends upon spiritual understanding; God deals with individuals, and everyone has a personal responsibility for his actions (Jeremiah xxxi. 29-34; compare Exodus xx. 5).

Judah becomes a client kingdom to Babylon, but later twice revolts (II Kings xxiv. 1, 17-20); Jerusalem falls and the inhabitants are carried into exile (II Kings xxv. 8-21).

Lessons of the Exile

During the Exile those who pondered upon the fate of the nation became convinced that God was universal, an idea which had already been suggested by Amos and Isaiah; together with this came a new and wider conception of the nation's mission, and a confirmation of belief in individual responsibility to God.

Ezekiel, prophet and priest, repeats Jeremiah's message of personal responsibility (Ezekiel xviii); the priests occupy a special position as being not merely, as hitherto regarded, guardians of holy places, but also of holy lives (iii. 18; xxxiv. 2-3, 11-12); men can avail themselves of the help of God's spirit to avoid sin (xi. 19-21; xxxvi. 26-27; xxxix. 29) which Ezekiel regards, like Isaiah, as a barrier to 'knowledge' of God (xiv. 1-6); in order to hold the Jews together during exile and prevent a dilution of their religion, Ezekiel emphasises the importance of keeping the Sabbath (xx. 12-13; xliv. 24) and builds up a new institutionalism (xl-xlviii).

In Isaiah xl-lv (written by an unknown author) there is an even more definite assertion of monotheism; other gods simply do not exist (Isaiah xl. 12-26; xliv. 6); the worship of idols is useless and absurd (xliv. 9-20). God desires the worship of all mankind (xlv. 22–24), but Gentile ideas of God are undeveloped so He has chosen Israel as His servant to be a missionary to all mankind (xlii. 1–12, xliii. 1–7), although the sin and blindness of the majority of the nation, even after the chastening of the exile, unfit them for the task (xlii. 18–25); nevertheless they shall be allowed to return to Jerusalem to carry out this mission as the 'Servant of the Lord' (xliii. 8–10; xlv. 1–7, 13); ritual is given a spiritual meaning (lviii), and the summit of Old Testament teaching about conduct is reached in the picture of suffering for others (xlii. 1–4; xlix. 1–6, l. 5–9; lii. 13–liii. 12).

The Return from Exile

The Jews who returned to Palestine experienced all the difficulties of a community that had been uprooted, transplanted and disorganised. Many of the abler and wealthier Jews did not return, at any rate at first. Under these circumstances it is not surprising that the repatriated exiles were wholly occupied in gaining a livelihood and reorganising their national and religious life. The prophets had protested against the conservatism of an established order, against the abuses of an organised society; after the return those 'zealous for the Lord' were mostly preoccupied with reconstruction and the re-establishment of institutional religion.

Haggai and Zechariah are concerned with the rebuilding of the Temple (Haggai i. 1–11; ii. 1–9) and of Jerusalem as the holy city (Zechariah ii. 1–6); Zechariah speaks of not only refraining from evil but also of the duty of not thinking evil in the heart (Zechariah vii. 8–14). The pattern of the religious life of the next 500 years is set by the adoption of Nehemiah's Law-book (Nehemiah viii. 1–8), and by the establishment of synagogues in every village as local meeting-places of worship in addition to the centralised religion of the Temple; they probably arose from the practice adopted during the Exile when no Temple was available. Ezra seeks to maintain the purity of Jewish religion by establishing it firmly on the basis of the Law (Ezra viii. 21–36). This gives rise to the body of commentators and exponents of the Law known as the Scribes. The office of high priest becomes important, and is made hereditary; the priests, from being members of the priestly family of Zadok, are called Zadokites or Sadducees, and from wealth acquired through the elaborate system of religious taxation, develop into a thoroughly worldly aristocracy.

As a result of this period the Jews become convinced that their destiny in God's purpose is not ended. By their faith in one God, and by obedience to His commandments, they can continue to be His people, a race distinct from others. The supreme teaching of Isaiah xl–lv—of God's mercy as universal, and of the people of God as being the servant of God for all nations—is not generally understood or accepted. The struggle to re-establish the Jewish nation in the face of difficulties, and the fear of contamination by the idolatrous and immoral ways of the Gentiles, leads to a narrow nationalism (Zechariah xiv. 12) and to Ezra's opposition to foreign marriages (Ezra x). Nevertheless, the noble universalistic ideal does not completely perish (Psalms xcvi; xcviii; c; Tobit xiii. 7–18; xiv. 6; Enoch x. 17–xi. 2); the story of Ruth is told as a counter to Ezra's opposition to foreign marriages. (The point of the story, that there was foreign blood in the royal family, is contained in the last verse of the book.) The parable story of Jonah asserts belief in God's care and mercy towards Israel's enemies.

Independence won and lost: Jewish hopes

After the conquests of Alexander the Great, the influence of Greek thought and the Greek way of life became strong among the Jews; the attraction of Greek philosophy began to weaken regard for the Law (cf. Ecclesiastes i; xii). Those who opposed this influence set out to uphold the strict observance of the Law, and from them arose those who became known as the Pharisees, or 'The Separate'. When Antiochus Epiphanes, who inherited the kingdom of Syria of which Palestine had become a part, tried to impose Greek ideas by force, the Jews resisted under the leadership of the Maccabees (I Maccabees ii–iv), and defended their religion by force of arms and diplomacy. This successful resistance to Gentile influences was followed by a period of aggressiveness and civil strife, ending in political subjection to Rome. These events led to a bitter nationalism, which found its extreme expression in the party of the Zealots, and to a belief that God must intervene; ideas as to how this was to happen were vague and varied; that probably most widely held was that a deliverer would arise in the person of a king of the house of David (St Matthew xxii. 41–42). The Early Church found these hopes fulfilled in Jesus of Nazareth, though he was not the Messiah the Jews had expected.

There grew up during these centuries new ideas about the after-life which are an advance upon the conception of a shadowy existence in Sheol; fellowship with God stronger than death (Job xiv. 13–15; Psalm xvi; lxxiii. 23–26; Song of Solomon viii. 6); belief in personal immortality (Wisdom ii. 23; iii. 1–9) and resurrection (Daniel xii. 2–3); these were the doctrines of the Pharisees but not of the Sadducees (Acts xxiii. 6–8).

III. STORIES FROM THE LIVES OF GREAT CHRISTIANS

'Moral education is impossible without the habitual vision of greatness.'   (WHITEHEAD.)

A good deal of religious teaching is necessarily about the Bible and about the historical setting of the events it relates. There is always a danger that this study of the Bible and its historical background may obscure the relevance of Christian teaching to modern times. To a child of eleven or twelve, 2000 years ago seems utterly remote; he cannot yet see that problems about God and Man and human conduct were then fundamentally the same as now, because nearly all the circumstances are different. Mrs George Brattle was expressing a common attitude in Trollope's *Vicar of Bullhampton* in saying: 'Them days and ours isn't the same', when refusing an invitation to show in her own life the spirit of the Master whom she professed to follow. It is therefore important to include stories from the lives of those great Christians who, right down to the present day, have dared to apply to the circumstances of their own generation the teaching and spirit of Jesus. Many of these stories appeal powerfully to children of this age, who may gain a deeper understanding of the teaching of Jesus from practical examples of action in circumstances with which they feel familiar than from the actual Gospel narrative set in the unfamiliar conditions of Palestine 2000 years ago.

It is suggested that it is better to interweave stories from the lives of great Christians with the story of the life of Jesus rather than to treat these stories as a separate piece of teaching. Most stories will be naturally introduced at various points in the course outlined on pp. 64–71; these points have not been there indicated, since it is considered best to leave to the teacher the selection of the precise moment in each case to suit his own manner of presentation. Teachers should also feel at liberty to 'work backwards', as it were, and refer to any action or saying recorded anywhere in the Gospels which can be regarded as being the example or inspiration of the life-story being considered.

The following list of names is by no means exhaustive or exclusive; there are many books available which give this type of material in convenient form. (A number are mentioned in the Book List on p. 175.) Teachers will continually be on the look-out for illustrative stories, particularly about men and women alive to-day. It does not matter that many children will already be familiar with the lives of some of those listed below, since their stories are of a quality which can bear repetition, and they all serve to illustrate the working of the spirit of Christ.

The references given are only some of those which can be used as the link with the life and teaching of Jesus, and the lives of many of these men and women are illustrations of more than one aspect of His teaching.

Brotherhood (St Mark iii. 31–35; St Luke x; xviii. 11–30)

William Penn.
Thomas Clarkson.
William Wilberforce.
Abraham Lincoln.
Booker Washington.
Dr Aggrey.

The Outcast (St Matthew xxv. 31–40; St Mark ii. 14–20; St Luke vii. 31–34)

Elizabeth Fry.
Dick Sheppard.
General Booth.
Toyohiko Kagawa.

Children (St Matthew xviii. 1–10)

Robert Raikes.
Lord Shaftesbury.
Dr Barnardo.

Healing (St Mark i. 29–45; St Matthew viii. 1–3, 6–17)

Rahere.

Dr John Addenbrooke.

Henri Dunant and the Red Cross.

Father Damien.

Sir Ronald Ross.

Madame Curie.

Albert Schweitzer.

Reformers (St Mark ii. 21, 22)

Wyclif.

Martin Luther.

John Huss.

John and Charles Wesley.

Missionaries (St Matthew xxviii. 19–20)

St Boniface.

John Williams.

Dr Grenfell.

Henry Martyn.

C. T. Studd.

Temple Gairdner.

Persecution (St John xv. 17–27)

Sir Thomas More.

Archbishop Cranmer.

Latimer and Ridley.

The Boy Martyrs of Uganda.

Pastor Niemöller.

Sacrifice (St Matthew xvi. 24–26; xix. 16–30; St John xv. 12–14)

Edward Wilson.

Captain Oates.

Alfred Sadd.

IV. Concerning the Bible

Owing to changes in the approach to the Bible brought about by critical study of the records, by recent archaeological discovery and by the development of general knowledge, it is important to familiarise pupils before they leave school with the main outline of the modern attitude towards the Bible, and to attempt a general introduction to its composition, contents and history. For, apart from the intrinsic value of such new knowledge, in no better way can children be forearmed against the attacks of shallow and pretentious scepticism which they must eventually meet. From such a course they should also begin to understand the ways of God towards men in his revelation of truth, and acquire a view of inspiration sounder than that which, with the best of intentions, reduced the Bible to an infallible reference book for verbatim guidance on life and conduct.

At the same time, while due weight should be assigned to these developments in our knowledge of the Bible and any questions raised be fairly faced, tentative or extreme hypotheses are better not mentioned, since they are liable to complicate the main theme and distract attention from the generally accepted findings of responsible scholarship. This point is emphasised because, in the violence of reaction against mechanical views of the Bible, harm has been done by the very extravagance of zeal in the other direction. In this way two attitudes, as unwarranted as they are to be regretted, have resulted. On the one hand, many have supposed that far more has been disturbed than is actually the case, so that they feel that the Bible is generally discredited; on the other hand, there are many in whom reaction has allied itself with unreasoning fears to resist any critical examination of the Scriptures on the ground that it imperils the very basis of religion.

Avoiding, therefore, any excess, the attempt should be made to impart to the pupils straightforward information as to how the Bible has reached them, and how, when and why the authors and compilers of the various books came to compose their work. This would naturally include a brief summary of the theme and contents of each book at its proper point in the sequence. Further, the pupil would be shown how these books came eventually to be collected into a Canon, or approved list, containing two 'Testaments'. Finally, certain simple and direct teaching is desirable, explaining, as far as is possible, what is to be understood by Revelation and the progressive nature of it; by Inspiration and the apparently varying degrees of it; and by the Authority of the Bible for life to-day, and the justification of it.

When we recognise that there are successive strata in the material which discloses the progressive revelation granted to inspired men of God, the Scriptures can be viewed as the record of the working out of a divine plan for one people, and through them for the world as a whole. The underlying unity of purpose will thus be brought out more vividly than was the case when all parts of the Bible were regarded as equally containing absolute truth communicated by God without regard either to human co-operation or human fallibility.

This course is drawn up so that it can be used in conjunction with the text-book *Concerning the Bible*, by Conrad Skinner,[1] which covers the same ground and in the same order. It treats the New Testament before the Old Testament throughout on the principle that boys and girls should be made familiar with the conception of God's character and action as revealed by Jesus Christ before the more partial conceptions and inevitable misconceptions of the earlier stages of revelation. But if any teacher prefers the chronological method the two sections of each part, being self-contained, can easily be interchanged. Such interchange is definitely recommended in the case of the Canon.

It is hardly necessary to add that for those who have the requisite knowledge the course can be taught without the use of this book, or with the use of material from other recommended books on the subject; in any case, at various points the teacher may wish to consult books which give a fuller treatment of particular aspects.

The course is so framed as to answer the following four major questions.

A. *Where did the Bible come from?*

Retrospect

It is recommended that the teacher should begin by undertaking a rapid retrospect, merely indicating the links that carry back the Revised Version to the original Scriptures. Such a retrospect is naturally suggested by the title-page of the Revised Version.

The Earliest Versions

As the actual originals are not available, and presumably no longer exist, there would here ensue a brief description of the earliest and most important authorities that have survived.

New Testament:

 (1) Greek manuscripts (copies in the original language, dating from the fourth and fifth centuries, and even, in fragmentary relics, from the second century).

[1] See Book List, p. 161.

(2) Versions (translations which in some cases are earlier than the existing Greek manuscripts).

(3) Writings of Early Fathers of the Church (some of which are earlier than either of the above categories) containing quotations from the New Testament.

It can be briefly indicated how, by comparison and deduction, it is possible to get back very close to the original text. This is the work of textual criticism—not the destructive activity of opponents, but the constructive work of devout minds.

Old Testament:

A similar procedure is suggested, though different in detailed application. It is possible to compare the main text as we have it to-day (in a tenth-century manuscript) with earlier but corrupted texts like the 'Samaritan Bible', and with famous versions such as the Septuagint and the Vulgate.

English Versions

A forward journey should now be undertaken, starting from the ancient documents and tracing in some detail the history and vicissitudes of the Bible in England from Anglo-Saxon days, with special attention to the following landmarks:

(1) Early English 'Bibles'. (For nearly twelve centuries up to 1539 the Vulgate stood as the authorised version of the whole Western Church.)

(2) Wyclif (the first complete Bible in English).

(3) Three important events between Wyclif and Tyndale:

(a) The invention of printing.

(b) The revival of learning.

(c) The Greek Testament of Erasmus.

(4) Tyndale.

(5) The Authorised Version (succeeding other versions, notably Coverdale's based on Tyndale).

(6) The Revised Version.

(7) Modern translations.

B.   *How did the various books in the Bible come to be written?*

New Testament

Into the story of the growth of the early Church are inserted, in their appropriate places, the various books of the New Testament.

(1) The beginnings of the Church. (Apostolic preaching and teaching.)

(2) The period of expansion. (Pauline epistles: formation of the oral tradition behind the Gospels.)

(3) The period of endurance and reflection, from Nero to Domitian. (I Peter; Hebrews; Revelation; the Synoptic Gospels; Acts.)

(4) The period of consolidation and interpretation. (II Peter; Jude; I, II, III John; James; the Fourth Gospel.)

Old Testament

One cannot speak of the date of many of the books of the Old Testament with the same degree of certainty as is possible with most of the New Testament. There were certain antecedent stages in the development of traditions which were later incorporated in literary form. Some idea should be given of:

(1) The common deposit (such as Hammurabi's Laws, Assyrian Flood Tablets).

(2) The lost books of the Hebrew chroniclers (such as the Book of the Wars of the Lord, the books of Jasher, Nathan, Iddo and Gad).

(3) Efforts at compilation: the meaning of the symbols J, E, D, P.

Because older material was frequently 'written up' from a later point of view, it is only possible to speak of the date of most books of the Old Testament 'in their present form'. For this reason it will probably be less confusing to allow the stages at which it is chosen to introduce the books to be, in most cases, those suggested by the material contained in them, rather than by the date of their composition, although this should also be indicated. In the following survey the emphasis should not be so much on the actual history, which has been treated in previous courses, as on the various books of the Old Testament which mark the stages and reflect the ideas belonging to that history.

(1) Early myths, legends and allegories (current in the Middle East before Abraham; material of Genesis i–xii; poetical fragments from Genesis to Judges).

(2) Beginnings of national consciousness (Abraham to Joshua; material of Genesis xiii–l, much of Exodus and Numbers, a little of Deuteronomy).

(3) Occupation of the Promised Land (Joshua; Judges; material of Ruth).

(4) Prophets and Kings (material of Samuel and Kings; the 'writing prophets', Amos, Hosea, Isaiah i–xxxix, Micah, Zephaniah, Nahum, Obadiah; the book of Deuteronomy).

(5) The Exile (Jeremiah; Ezekiel, who partially combines the functions of prophet and priest; Isaiah xl–lv; Leviticus; editing of Kings and Samuel).

(6) After the exile (supremacy of priests; Ezra–Nehemiah, originally one book; final editing of Genesis, Exodus, Numbers, Leviticus, Deuteronomy, Joshua, Judges; prophets, such as Haggai and Zechariah, fewer and appearing at rarer intervals; Chronicles, Malachi and Job; the material of Esther; Psalms and Ruth in their present form, and possibly Proverbs and Lamentations).

(7) The last three centuries (Joel; Ecclesiastes; Song of Songs; Jonah; the impact of the Greeks on the Jews; Daniel; apocryphal books, such as Maccabees and Ecclesiasticus; Esther probably written at this time).

C. *How did the various books come to be collected into the Old and New Testaments? What governed their selection?*

In this section it is recommended that the Old Testament should be considered before the New Testament. Although the subject should not be treated in laborious detail, it has a logical place in the course. One cannot speak of the inspiration of the books of the Bible without dealing with the question of the selection of those books which were considered to be inspired. In the case of the Old Testament the Jews adopted what we should now consider certain arbitrary standards in fixing the Canon. In the case of the New Testament the early Church, in granting authority for the reading of the new 'Scriptures' in church, or in admitting their validity for establishing points of doctrine, did not consider that a new Canon was being set up to supplement the Old Testament.

The Old Testament Canon

Although some authorities maintain that the canonicity of all the books was first declared about A.D. 100, two of the three quite separate sections, into which the Old Testament Canon falls, received acceptance at an earlier date.

(1) The Law (Genesis, Exodus, Leviticus, Numbers, Deuteronomy) first accepted under Ezra 397 B.C.

(2) The Prophets (Joshua, Judges, Samuel and Kings— history written from the prophetic standpoint, and called the 'Former' prophets; and Isaiah, Jeremiah, Ezekiel, Hosea, Joel, Amos, Obadiah, Jonah, Micah, Nahum, Habbakuk, Zephaniah, Haggai, Zechariah and Malachi, comprising the 'Latter' prophets) accepted by 165 B.C.

(3) The Writings (Psalms, Proverbs, Job, Song of Songs, Ruth, Lamentations, Ecclesiastes, Esther, Daniel, Ezra, Nehemiah, Chronicles) established in the first century A.D.

The Apocrypha

These books were not included in the Canon of the Hebrew Old Testament, but passed from the Greek version of the Old Testament into the Christian Church.

The New Testament Canon

Some twenty books had secured unquestionable recognition before A.D. 200. The completion of the Canon was achieved by a slow process, but the ultimately rejected books were never formed into a secondary Canon or collection like the Old Testament Apocrypha.

D. *What is there unique about the Books of the Bible?*

Before abstract words such as 'Revelation', 'Inspiration' and 'Authority' are used in relation to the Bible it is well to recall the picture of the Bible as a whole as the record of the progressive disclosure of God's nature and purpose. The revelation is to living men who are themselves inspired to receive it, and it is the message thus communicated by God which carries authority. A distinction must often be made between the man who originally received the revelation and the man who recorded it; failure to do so has in the past led to the worship of the letter and to false theories of infallibility.

Revelation

Revelation cannot be confined to the Bible, nor can every passage of the Bible, taken by itself, be equally regarded as a vehicle of revelation; but taken as a whole, the Bible is unique in its unwavering witness to God's continual dealings with a people in the unfolding of a single purpose.

Inspiration

The human recipients of revelation were inspired to receive God's message, and it was this which distinguished them from their fellows and which makes the Bible unique. A recognition of the uniqueness of the Bible record has sometimes led to theories of verbal inspiration which seem to have gone astray in imposing a theory on the facts of the Bible instead of deriving one from them.

Authority

The claim which the Bible thus makes upon us to-day (but not separated from the present activity of the Holy Spirit in leading us into truth) is that it is the record of proven spiritual experiences in the lives of men, and of how they were inspired to receive revelation beyond the power of mere reason to acquire.

V. THE UNIVERSAL GOSPEL

It is hoped that all children, before they leave school, will be given some idea of the manner in which Christianity reached England and of subsequent developments. For children who leave school at fifteen, a little less time may be spent on the course 'Concerning the Bible', in order to allow time for a condensed and simplified form of the course 'Unto All the World: the Universal Gospel' on pp. 90–94.

CHILDREN AGED 15

I. UNTO ALL THE WORLD: THE UNIVERSAL GOSPEL

From Jerusalem to Rome

A brief revision of the work covered on pp. 70–71 will recapitulate the spread of the Gospel from Palestine through Syria, Asia Minor and Greece to Rome.

The Evangelisation of the Roman Empire

Except for Paul and the accounts of his missionary journeys, little is known of the men and women who carried the Gospel throughout the Roman Empire. Christianity spread along the great trade routes of the Empire; this evangelisation appears to have been the work of ordinary Christians as they went about their normal business. (In this and the following sections, H. Bettenson's *Documents of the Christian Church* will be found a useful source-book).

The Persecution of Christianity by the Empire

The Roman Empire on the whole pursued a policy of religious toleration; Christianity was persecuted either as likely to interfere with this religious toleration or, more often, because Christians regarded the Empire as transitory and refused absolutely to recognise its authority in any matter affecting their way of living; for them, this was governed uncompromisingly by the teaching of Jesus alone.

> The beginnings of persecution (Hebrews x. 32–34; I Peter ii. 19–25; iv. 12–16).
>
> The martyrs: the book of Revelation as a pamphlet of an 'underground movement' (Revelation vi. 9–11; vii. 13–17; xxi. 1–7, 22–27).
>
> Persecution under Nero and Domitian.
>
> Correspondence between Trajan and Pliny.
>
> Persecution under Decius and Diocletian.

The Victory of the Church

The Church is recognised by the Empire under Constantine. The victory was won by heroic faith and courage. It was not all gain. Religion often thrives better on persecution than on patronage. What conquered paganism was not Christianity but an institution called the Christian Church—and rightly so called because it did on the whole derive its inspiration from Christ. The Church made the Empire Christian; but when the Church already contained elements that were not Christian, and much that was pharisaical, there was always the danger of the Empire making the Church pagan. On the whole the gain outweighed the loss; the imperial Church, with all its failings, did save Christian civilisation. The subsequent history of the Church is the story of the struggle of the better elements in it to make the Church more truly Christian.

In the sections which follow use should be made, where possible, of local history, to illustrate the story of Christianity in this country. It is an excellent thing when these lessons take the form of excursions to places and buildings in the neighbourhood which are associated with this story, or where it can be illustrated from the lives of local men and women.[1]

The Establishment of Christianity in Britain

The unknown missionaries during the Roman occupation.
The martyrdom of Alban.
The mission from Ireland; Patrick, Columba, Aidan.
The mission of Augustine.
The Synod of Whitby.

The Medieval Church in England

A study of the medieval Church is impossible without some reference to the life and work of the monasteries. An unbiased view of monasticism is not easy to find, yet, in spite of perversions and corruptions, at its best it did preserve the Christian tradition and give expression to important Christian ideals in an ignorant and turbulent world.

The religious life of medieval England may be examined as represented by one of the great monastic orders or by the coming

[1] In Cambridgeshire, *Christianity in Southern Fenland*, by R. F. McNeile, will be found useful.

of the Friars; carefully chosen selections from *Piers Plowman* may also provide useful material.

The Reformation

The Reformation was not only a protest against certain grave abuses which had crept into the life and teaching of the Church: it was a positive restatement of the Christian message. It was not an appeal to new ideas but to the Gospel, and because of this it reasserted rather than broke the true continuity of the Church.

The work and influence of Erasmus.

Continental movements; Luther and Calvin.

English Christianity under the impact of the continental movements; tension between them and the medieval tradition; the English Bible and the Book of Common Prayer; the Elizabethan settlement.

The influence of Calvinism; Puritans, Presbyterians and Independents; Baptists; the Society of Friends.

The settlements of 1662 and 1668; the Established Church; Catholic recusants; Protestant dissenters.

Movements of English Christianity

Within the history of Christianity in England since the Reformation there have been two great religious movements, that of Wesley and the Evangelicals in the eighteenth century, and that of the Tractarians in the nineteenth century. Both illustrate and emphasise certain essential aspects of religion which were in grave danger of being forgotten.

The Evangelical Revival

John Wesley, Charles Simeon; Charles Wesley and hymns of the period; Robert Raikes and the Sunday School movement.

The Oxford Movement

Keble, Pusey, Newman; revival of the sacramental life.

The Christian Social Movement

Wilberforce and the abolition of slavery; Shaftesbury and the factory laws; Elizabeth Fry and prison reform; Charles Kingsley, F. D. Maurice, Charles Gore, H. Scott Holland.

The Revival of Missionary Enterprise

The Christian Church in this country in the early days was a missionary Church, as can be seen from the continental missions of Boniface and Gall. In the Middle Ages the Church in England shared in the general missionary work of the Western Church. By the end of the seventeenth century there was the beginning of a new era of missionary enterprise with the foundation of the great Missionary Societies.

The story of the missionary work of the Church is best told in the form of stories of individual missionaries. Some of these will already be familiar from ' Stories from the Lives of Great Christians' (pp. 80–82); details of the work of others may be found in the books mentioned in the Book List on p. 175.

Movements towards Reunion

In the present century the most notable feature in the life of the Christian Church throughout the world, arising in the first place largely as the outcome of missionary work, has been the growing emphasis upon its essential unity despite the almost innumerable 'churches', denominations and sects into which it is, superficially, divided. Since older children often find the divisions of the Church a very real stumbling-block, and regard them as a 'scandal', it is desirable that they should learn something of the efforts which have been made, with a large measure of success, to realise and demonstrate the unity of Christians throughout the world, whatever their race, nationality, class or denomination. The history of this 'oecumenical movement' is largely a story of successive world conferences.

> The World Missionary Conference at Edinburgh in 1910.
> Out of this arose the International Missionary Council, which met at Jerusalem in 1928 and at Tambaram, Madras, in 1938.
> Conferences on 'Faith and Order' at Lausanne in 1927 and at Edinburgh in 1937.
> Conferences on 'Life and Work' at Stockholm in 1925 and at Oxford in 1937.

World Conferences of Christian Youth at Amsterdam in 1939 and at Oslo in 1947.

The formation of the World Council of Churches, meeting at Amsterdam in 1948.

Since, however, it may not be easy to present a record of conferences in such a way as to appeal to the interest and imagination even of older children, it may be better to present this movement through the work of notable individual leaders, like Robert H. Gardiner and John R. Mott of the U.S.A., Archbishop Soderblom of Sweden, and, not least, Archbishop William Temple in this country. As a result of their labours there is now in existence a World Council of Churches which gives practical and effective expression to the reality of a world-wide Christian fellowship which transcends the divisions that separate men from one another. A practical example of what can be achieved by sustained and earnest endeavour to emphasise essential unity and subordinate differences can be seen in the union of churches in South India.[1]

Information about the rise and progress of the movement toward reunion can be found most easily in *The Ecumenical Movement*[2] by H. G. G. Herklots and in *A Christian Year Book*.[3]

II. PERSONAL AND CORPORATE RELIGION

Scattered throughout the pages of the New Testament is a great deal of teaching concerning both personal and corporate religion. These have been grouped together under headings to make a course designed to help boys and girls to understand more of these two aspects of religion. For the sake of clearness the two sides, personal and corporate, are set out separately, although in the teaching they should probably be interwoven.

It is natural that the subject of prayer occupies a place of importance. The opportunity should be taken to teach as much about prayer as can be understood by boys and girls of this age.

[1] A useful account of this is contained in the pamphlet *South India's New Church*, by C. S. Milford (Edinburgh House Press, 1947).

[2] Christian Discussion Groups Pamphlet No. 14, published by the National Society and the Society for Promoting Christian Knowledge, 1947.

[3] Student Christian Movement Press, 1947.

The subject was dealt with in the Junior Course, but it can now be approached from a more adult point of view, and it will be possible to deal with the particular difficulties experienced by adolescents.

Personal Religion

The call to personal religion

(1) John the Baptist's scorn of an institutionalism devoid of personal reality (St Matthew iii. 7–12). Our Lord repeats the Baptist's preaching. His term is 'hypocrites'— 'actors' (St Matthew vi. 2–5; xv. 7; xxiii. 14; xxiv. 51).

(2) Our Lord's call to the individual.
The individual call (St Mark i. 16–20; ii. 14), individual conversion (St Matthew xviii. 3; St Luke xxii. 32), praise of individual faith (St Mark v. 25–34; St Luke vii. 2–9), individual self-renunciation (St Mark x. 17–22), the individual cross (St Matthew xvi. 24; St Luke xiv. 27–33), the new birth of the individual (St John iii. 1–5), the spiritual food of the individual (St John iv. 14; vi. 47–58).

(3) Our Lord and private prayer.
His practice (St Luke iii. 21; v. 16; vi. 12; ix. 18, 28; xi. 1; xxii. 41). His teaching (St Matthew vi. 6; St Luke xviii. 1–5, 9–14).

(4) Paul.
His personal conversion (Acts ix), his personal call—a call from God, not men (Galatians i. 11–24), his insistence that without the Spirit of Christ there is no Christian discipleship (Romans viii. 9–14), his mission to individuals (Acts xx. 20; Philemon), his private prayers (Romans i. 9; Ephesians iii. 14; Philippians i. 4; II Timothy i. 16–18).

The foundations of personal religion

(1) Personal faith in God.
Our Lord's own supreme faith.
His constant reliance upon the unfailing purposes of God in His own life (St Luke ii. 49; St John iv. 34; ix. 4;

95

x. 28–30; St Luke xxiii. 46), the faith which He teaches (St Matthew xvii. 19–21; St Mark xi. 22), the faith of His disciples (Romans viii. 31; I Corinthians xv. 10; I Timothy iv. 10).

(2) Personal faith in Jesus Christ.

The faith of the disciples (Acts xvi. 31; II Corinthians v. 14; Philippians iv. 13); personal love for Jesus is common to all true Christians (St John xx. 11–16; xxi. 15; I Peter i. 8), but the early Christians did not dwell so much on their love for Jesus—there was no wonder in that—as on the wonder of Christ's love for them (I John iv. 10–19; Galatians ii. 20), so that their love became adoration (St John xx. 28).

(3) The result in personal conduct.

The great commandment (St Matthew xxii. 35–40).

Our love of God: first and fundamental.

Our love of our neighbours, like ourselves, the children of God.

Two great warnings: against vindictiveness (St Matthew v. 43–48; xviii. 23–35), and against acquisitiveness (St Matthew vi. 19–24. The 'single eye' is single-hearted service to God).

Corporate Religion

The call to corporate religion

(1) Personal religion a way into the Kingdom (St Matthew v. 20; vii. 21; xviii. 3; St Mark ix. 47; xii. 34; St Luke ix. 62).

(2) The call of the group.

The choice of the Twelve (St Mark iii. 14), their mission (St Mark vi. 7–13); many sheep, one flock (St John x. 16); the Last Supper: 'the Communion' and the new covenant (St Matthew xxvi. 26–28); the one vine and its branches (St John xv. 1–5), the prayer for unity (St John xvii. 9–21), the final commission to the disciples, not the Twelve only (St John xx. 21; St Matthew xxviii. 19–20).

(3) Our Lord and corporate prayer.

His practice (St Luke iv. 16, 33; vi. 6), His teaching
(St Matthew vi. 9–13; xviii. 19–20).

(4) Paul.

Joins with other Christians (Acts ix. 19, 26–28), his care
for the group (Acts xiv. 22–23; xx. 17–32), his appeal for
unity (I Corinthians i. 10–13; Ephesians iv. 1–16), his
letters to churches.

The foundations of corporate religion

(1) The corporate faith of the Church.

The primary confession, 'Jesus is Lord' (Romans x. 9;
I Corinthians xii. 3; Philippians ii. 11).

Foundations of faith; the Cross (I Corinthians i. 23–25;
Galatians ii. 20; vi. 14; Philippians ii. 6–8), the Resurrection—historic fact (I Corinthians xv. 1–11, 19–21;
Philippians ii. 9), new power (Philippians iii. 10), new
life (Romans vi. 4; Colossians iii. 1–4)—Pentecost; the
power and witness of the Spirit (Acts ii. 1–4; v. 32;
Romans xv. 13, 19; I Corinthians ii. 1–5; I Thessalonians
i. 5). On these experiences the Church gradually formulated its faith. But behind all this lay the ancient faith in
God. It is God who gave His Son (St John iii. 16), God
who raised Him from the dead (Acts ii. 32; x. 40),
God who gives the Spirit (St Luke xi. 13; Acts v. 32),
God from whose love nothing can separate us (Romans
viii. 39). Christianity begins, not with Christ, but with
God in Christ (II Corinthians v. 19); many wrong conceptions of God have arisen from forgetting this.

(2) The corporate worship of the Church.

Its essential character is already seen at the beginning in
Jerusalem (Acts ii. 42); instruction, prayer and sacrament
are clearly included. These continue side by side in the
development of the Church. Instruction is everywhere—
in preaching and in letters. Emphasis is laid on growth
(I Peter ii. 2; II Peter iii. 18; Ephesians iv. 11–15;
I Thessalonians iv. 1; Philippians iii. 12–14). There is
seldom need to mention corporate prayer; it is assumed

(Acts xii. 5; xvi. 13). The continuance of sacraments is likewise assumed.

It is important to keep the balance of the New Testament. In the complete picture of Christianity as there described, both exhortation and teaching, baptism and the Lord's Supper form an essential part.

Baptism (Acts ii. 38; viii. 12, 36–38; x. 47; xvi. 33; Romans vi. 3–4; I Corinthians xii. 13; I Peter iii. 21); sometimes followed by the laying on of the Apostles' hands (Acts viii. 17; xix. 5–6).

The Lord's Supper. Its institution (St Matthew xxvi. 26–28; St Luke xxii. 19–20; I Corinthians xi. 23–26); probably described at first as 'the breaking of bread' (Acts ii. 42, 46; compare St Luke xxiv. 35), then as 'the Lord's Supper' (I Corinthians xi. 20).

Other aspects of Christian worship (I Corinthians xii. 4–31; xiv. 23–40; Ephesians v. 19–20).

The place of meeting; in the early days, as sometimes in the modern mission field, the Christian community often assembled in the houses of its members (Acts xviii. 7; xix. 9; xx. 7–8; Colossians iv. 15; Romans xvi. 3–5; Philemon 2).

'The Lord's Day'—the weekly memorial of the Resurrection (Acts xx. 7; I Corinthians xvi. 2, Revelation i. 10).

(3) The corporate life of the Church.

This was an immediate outcome of Pentecost; those who shared the gift of the Spirit felt themselves at once linked together in one fellowship (Acts ii).

The unity of the Church; the wrongfulness of division (I Corinthians iii. 3–7; Philippians ii. 1–4), the one body and the many members (Romans xii. 3–21; I Corinthians xii; Ephesians i. 15–23; ii. 19–22; iii. 14–21; iv. 1–16), practical expression in Paul's collection for the poor Christians of Jerusalem (Romans xv. 26; I Corinthians xvi. 1–3; II Corinthians viii, ix) and the mutual love and care for their fellows which distinguished the Christians (Romans xii. 9–20; I Corinthians xiii; I Peter iii. 8–9; I John iii. 14–18; iv. 20–21).

ALTERNATIVE COURSE FOR CHILDREN AGED 11–15

It will be recognised that a great deal of the foregoing syllabus is unsuitable for some children. Teachers may be able to adapt it to suit the requirements of these children, but it has been felt that there are some children who need something simpler. It is suggested that a minimum which might be attempted would be the following:

Children aged 11–13:

A simple life of Christ, based on the synoptic Gospels.
Stories of heroes and prophets of the Old Testament, their achievements, mistakes and endeavours to serve God.

Children aged 13–15:

The growth of Christianity, from the Apostles to modern times.
The Christian way of life and its application to modern life and problems.
The Bible Library and a simple history of the English Bible.

Some suggestions as to how this outline could be covered are made below. The minds of some children are very immature and questions which cause unnecessary conflicts in their minds, such as certain miracles, or the 'Chosen People', should be avoided. Instead the teacher should try to give the child simple, positive rules of conduct based on the life and teaching of Jesus and illustrated with examples from the Old Testament (where, sometimes, the example is by contrast) to the present day. The work must be simple, yet dramatic, colourful and vivid; pictures and illustrations of all kinds should be used. Interest must be personal, not conceptual; it must be centred on real people, and be closely linked with things the child understands and the life he knows.

Teachers who use this course should nevertheless be familiar with the standard course, the material of which may in many instances be of use to the teacher who is giving a simpler presentation.

7-2

CHILDREN AGED 11–13

The Story of the Life of Jesus

Stories of Jesus' birth

The Annunciation (St Luke i. 26–35), the Magnificat (St Luke i. 46–55), the shepherds (St Luke ii. 1–20), the kings (St Matthew ii. 1–12), the flight into Egypt (ii. 13–23); carols and nativity plays.

His Boyhood

The child in the Temple (St Luke ii. 40–50), gifted and popular (St Luke ii. 52).

What may be learnt of His home and surroundings:

Roman government. Interference with ordinary life (census, St Luke ii. 1–3; forced labour, St Matthew v. 41), tribute money (St Matthew xxii. 17), Roman officers (St Mark x. 42–43), tax-gatherers (St Matthew ix. 9; St Luke xix. 1–10). The house He lived in—one room? (St Matthew v. 15; St Luke viii. 16; xi. 5–8).

The food He ate. Cakes of oil and meal (I Kings xvii. 12–13), leavened bread (St Matthew xiii. 33), parched corn and cheese (I Samuel xvii. 17–18), figs, raisins, meat, wine (I Samuel xxv. 18), honey (I Samuel xiv. 25–30), fish (St John xxi. 3–13), loaves and fishes (St Mark vi. 35–44).

Games He played (St Luke vii. 32).

His family (St Matthew xiii. 54–56).

School and synagogue. Sand writing (St John viii. 6), tablets (St Luke i. 63), rolls (Jeremiah xxxvi. 1–8, 20–32; St Luke iv. 16–20); psalms He learnt by heart, 'The Lord is my shepherd' (Psalm xxiii), the Song of the Seasons (Psalm lxv. 1–2, 8–13), Evening Hymn (Psalm cxxxiv), Hymn of Praise (Psalms cxlvii–cl).

What He saw in the countryside. The hills and fields (Psalm civ. 1, 5–18), flowers (St Matthew vi. 28–30), fledgelings fallen from the nest (St Matthew x. 29), weather lore (St Matthew xvi. 2–3).

Jesus' Friends

His disciples (St Matthew iv. 18–22; St Luke v. 1–11, 27–32
St John i. 43–50), the family at Bethany (St Luke x. 38–42;
St John xi. 1–46; xii. 1–8), Zacchaeus (St Luke xix. 1–9),
Nicodemus (St John iii. 1–10; vii. 50–52; xix. 39–40),
'certain women' (St Luke viii. 1–3, 23, 27, 49).

His Work

Healing:

Simon's mother-in-law (St Mark i. 29–45), the sick of the
palsy (St Luke v. 18–26), the ten lepers (St Luke xvii. 11–19),
healing the blind (St Luke xviii. 35–43), Jairus' daughter (St
Mark v. 22–43), the centurion's servant (St Luke vii. 2–10).

Teaching—from people and things He saw around Him:

The farmer and his soil (St Matthew xiii. 3–8), weeds in the
wheat (St Matthew xiii. 24–30), farm-labourers (St Matthew
xx. 1–16), growing seed (St Mark iv. 26–29), vine-pruners
(St John xv. 1–6), the lost sheep (St Luke xv. 3–7), the good
shepherd (St John x. 1–16), fishermen (St Luke v. 1–11), the
builder (St Luke vi. 46–49), an industrial accident (St Luke
vi. 41–42).

Parties: the great supper (St Luke xiv. 15–24), the wedding
at Cana (St John ii. 1–11), bridesmaids (St Matthew xxv.
1–13), the particular Pharisee (St Luke xi. 37–39), the
unmannerly Pharisee (St Luke vii. 36–50).

Jesus and God

Prayer in the mountain (St Luke vi. 12–19), how to pray
(St Matthew vi. 1–15), Jesus' prayer in Gethsemane (St Mark
xiv. 32–42), repentance (St Luke xv), doing more than is
required (St Matthew v. 43–48).

Jesus in Danger

Loyalty declared by Thomas (St John xi. 8–16), and Peter
(St Mark xiv. 27–31); the Last Supper and the arrest (St
Matthew xxvi. 1–5, 14–58, 69–75).

Suffering and Triumph

The Crucifixion (St Luke xxii. 63–xxiii. 47), the empty tomb (St Luke xxiv. 1–12), Emmaus (St Luke xxiv. 13–35), Thomas convinced (St John xx. 24–28).

After Pentecost. 'Go ye into all the world.'

The inspiration of the Holy Spirit (Acts ii. 1–13), the first preaching of the Gospel (Acts ii. 14–20), the fellowship of believers (Acts ii. 41–47), healing in Jesus' name (Acts iii. 1–10), the courage of Peter and John (Acts iv. 1–22), Jesus' followers at prayer (Acts iv. 23–31), community of goods (Acts iv. 32–37).

Heroes of the Old Testament: stories Jesus heard and books He read

Abraham. His call (Genesis xii. 1–5), his treatment of Lot (Genesis xiii. 1–12), the promise made to him (Genesis xiii. 14–17), his faith (Genesis xxii. 1–19).

Jacob and Esau. Jacob's sin against Esau (Genesis xxv. 29–34; xxvii. 1–40; xxviii. 1–5, 10–22), his exile (Genesis xxvii. 41–45), his return and reunion with Esau (Genesis xxxii. 3–22; xxxiii. 1–17).

Joseph and his brethren. (Genesis xxxvii; xxxix. 1–6; xli–xlvi. 7.)

Moses. The deliverer (Exodus iii), the exodus (Exodus xiii; xiv; xvi; xvii. 1–7), the Covenant and the Ten Commandments (Exodus xix. 1–6; xx. 1–17).

Joshua. The settlement of Canaan (Numbers xxvii. 15–23; Joshua iii; vi).

Gideon. The valiant three hundred (Judges vi. 1–24; vii).

Samuel. His call (I Samuel ii. 1–11; iii); anointing of Saul (I Samuel ix–x. 1).

David. The slaying of Goliath (I Samuel xvii), his friendship with Jonathan (I Samuel xviii. 1–4; xix. 1–7; xx; II Samuel i), his sparing of Saul (I Samuel xxiv), kindness to Jonathan's son (II Samuel ix).

Solomon. His wisdom (I Kings ii. 1–4; iii. 5–28); the House of the Lord (I Kings v; vi. 7; viii. 62–66), the Queen of Sheba (I Kings x. 1–13).

Heroes and prophets of the dark days

Incidents should be chosen and treated simply from the life and work of Elijah, Elisha, Amos, Isaiah, Jeremiah, Nehemiah and Ezra.

CHILDREN AGED 13–15

The Life and Teaching of Christ

The world to which Jesus came

An attempt should be made to give some idea of the later developments of Judaism into the form in which our Lord found it, in order that there may be a better understanding of His life and teaching.

> The return from exile; Nehemiah rebuilding the walls; Ezra giving the law.
> The story of Judas Maccabaeus.
> Conquest by the Romans and the capture of Jerusalem in 63 B.C. Jewish hopes, born of distress, for a Ruler and Deliverer of His people.

The Story of the Life of Jesus (revision)

The Growth of Christianity

Peter. Friendship with Jesus, courage after Pentecost (revision), experience with Cornelius (Acts x).

Persecution. Stephen (Acts vi. 9–15; vii. 54–60), Philip (Acts viii. 1–6).

Paul. Conversion (Acts ix. 1–25), reluctant acceptance by the apostles (Acts ix. 26–33). Missionary journeys, in Galatia (Acts xiv; Galatians i. 1–10; iv. 12–20); in Philippi (Acts xvi; Philippians i. 1–11; iv. 4–23); in Corinth (Acts xviii; I Corinthians i. 1–17; xiii); in Ephesus (Acts xix; Ephesians ii. 13–22; vi. 10–20); journey to Rome and shipwreck (Acts xxvii); at Rome (Acts xxviii).

The Early Church. The catacombs; Constantine; stories of early martyrs such as St George.

Christianity Spreads to Britain. Early saints and teachers, such as St Patrick, St Columba, St Aidan, St Augustine, St Edmund, St Alban and others. The monasteries and the friars. Wyclif and the Lollards. Luther and religious freedom. The Quaker movement. The Wesleys and Methodism. Booth and the Salvation Army. Modern missionary movements.

Christianity and its application to modern life and problems

The section on pp. 80–82 on 'Stories from the Lives of Great Christians' will be found suitable in its present form.

The Bible

A very much simplified version of the course 'Concerning the Bible' on pp. 82–89 can be used. Many of the details of this course will be omitted, but it will be possible to convey a broad picture of the Bible as a library of books of greatly differing age and value, and an outline of the main steps by which the English Bible has reached us from the original manuscripts.

THE SIXTH FORM

It has been felt wise to endow the syllabus for the sixth form with even greater freedom and flexibility than those suggested for younger age-groups, not only because conditions vary so greatly between the sixth forms of school and school, but also because so much depends upon the particular teacher. At first a teacher may lean towards precedent and a firmly marked track, and, perhaps nervous in a strange world, be grateful for a wealth of detail and a systematic course fully worked out. Later, however, the teacher will realise that he can build on his own experience. For this reason there will be found in the following pages two courses worked out in some detail, followed by a number of suggestions or indications of lines of approach, which the teacher who has the necessary equipment may be glad to follow. One thing is certain; religious teaching should be on a level with other subjects, in the sense that doubt, question and discussion should play as big a part in it as they do in a lesson on history or biology. So long as religious teaching implicitly demands the acceptance of tradition as such and denies the right to question it, so long it is bound, nowadays, to fail.

While for no age-group should a syllabus function as a cage or mould of uniformity, certainly for the sixth form it should be designed rather as a spring-board, a liberation from a narrow conception of the teacher's task. Stephen Leacock writes of the man who leapt upon a horse and 'rode off madly in all directions'. Symptoms of just such a centrifugal phenomenon may be observable in the approach to the sixth form syllabus which follows. It has been necessary to provide a horse suitable for those who have none, for those who find themselves not yet at home in the saddle, or for those who have no strong sense of direction; even the free-lance Quixote, with predetermined objectives and accustomed to his well-trained Rosinante, may become a more experienced horseman after a canter on another steed. Our horse, clearly, cannot be a Pegasus, but neither must he be a mere Dobbin; he should have something of the quality of that Leacockian steed—a capacity to take a variety of roads simultaneously! This provision of a number of tracks towards the same goal is designed to correspond to the diversity of approach which is found among those engaged in sixth form religious teaching.

There is a division to be observed between those who look upon sixth form religious instruction primarily as Scripture teaching, and those who regard it as the delineation of Christian faith and life. Within each of these groups there is again a division formed by the difference between what might be called the 'direct' and 'indirect' approach, between those who make the Bible or the Christian faith their starting point and those who start from the pupils in front of them. The two approaches are not beyond being harmonised; in fact, in every teacher, they have to come to terms, but there are real distinctions in the choice and degree of emphasis accorded.

Among those who look upon their task as being in the first place the teaching of Scripture there are some who feel that, before any opinion worthy of the name can be formed by a pupil, he must be grounded securely in the requisite basic knowledge; they will take a roving course over the Bible and its contemporary environment, the development of its religious ideas and its records of recognised acts of God. Others feel compelled to get to grips at once with the doubts, difficulties and perversities of later adolescence; they are aware of an overriding necessity to grapple with this unexamined and often uninformed antagonism, which, they feel, if ignored, can vitiate the transfer of the most excellent material by the ablest teacher. These aver that they must begin at the class end, and, if possible, establish a starting point in the knowledge and experience of religion already consciously or unconsciously possessed; from this it will be possible to proceed according to a centripetal rather than a distributive programme. The choice of this method is exacting, for it means that progress along a general line, which may be firmly in the mind and intention of the teacher, must be subject to endless interruptions and detours; but just because of these, it may prove in the end to be far more valuable than a quite orderly procession along a predetermined route.

Among those, again, who regard sixth form religious teaching as the exposition of the Christian faith and life, one teacher will take the corpus of Christian truth, the deposit of faith, and present it with sincere fidelity in, say, an expansion of the Apostles' Creed, trusting to win both understanding and acceptance. Another feels that the first imperative is to disperse the collections of half-baked ideas and almost total misconceptions which obsess the minds of his pupils and prevent the inflow of truth. Having secured a foothold among them and by frankness established a bond of confidence, he will proceed from this periphery of general beliefs and ideas and work inwards towards the same goal as the other man—a knowledge of Christ and an understanding of the Christian way of living.

Whatever course is followed, and whatever approach the teacher uses, two things must be attempted. The first is to introduce boys and girls to the 'historical authentication' of the Gospel. The critical discoveries of the last generation have left a far surer historical basis than was ever anticipated when the movement began. Every member of a sixth form should be given the opportunity to realise how difficult it is for the historian to interpret Mark, or the common ground of Matthew and Luke, as anything other than history, in the sense that Plutarch's *Alexander*, or even Tacitus' *Agricola*, is history. The other essential is to make clear the limitations of materialism, or at least to discuss them. Perhaps the best statement of these limitations is still to be found in Plato's *Phaedo*, 97 C–99 D, although it has been attempted many times since. It is important at the same time to emphasise what is still to be achieved by the application of mechanistic conceptions; without them we can get no further in science. But it is equally clear that the limitations of science should in general terms be understood. One reason for past failures in schools has been the cleavage between science and the humanities; schoolmasters whose stock-in-trade was the humanities once decried science openly, and scientists were not unnaturally eager to decry humane studies. So long as this continues to happen, a balanced view can never be formed in a school.

Although there can be no falser or more perilous attitude than that which sets the academic or the critical in opposition to the devotional, confining the one to the classroom and the other to the chapel or the assembly for worship, the general approach to sixth form religious teaching should nevertheless be intellectual rather than devotional. The immediate aim of the teacher is not to evoke a direct assent from members of the class, but to present to them the Christian faith as something as much based on fact and as much a subject for intellectual scrutiny as any other. Yet the ultimate object will not be the mere conveyance of information to the pupil's mind, but the educating of his faculties of comprehension, analysis, and, in the end, decision.

A syllabus, however, must be a course of study. Whatever the approach the course must aim at giving a systematic knowledge of the Christian way of living, and an understanding of the historical basis on which it is founded. The value of the course taken lies not magically in itself but in the opportunity it provides for the spiritual development of the individual who is willing to appropriate it. It cannot constitute more than an opportunity—spiritual development cannot be forced. Furthermore, it probably remains true that, whatever the syllabus, the character of the school's community life, together with the 'witness to the faith' of respected masters and mistresses, will be the greater influence. When they reach the sixth form of a secondary school, boys and girls for the first time begin to have a respect for intellectual capacity. To see an adult, whose intellect in other fields is respected or admired, professing the Christian faith and manifestly guiding his actions in accordance with the Christian way of life, commends Christianity to the older adolescent even more than an able exposition of doctrine. This influence often operates with greater power in others than in the Scripture teacher, since to some extent a profession of Christianity is regarded as part of the Scripture teacher's business. For this reason, while the teacher of Scripture with 'specialist' knowledge is in many ways desirable, his position is strengthened if his teaching includes other subjects as well. For the same reason the more men and women of Christian profession, distinguished in the world outside, whom a sixth form can meet and hear, the better.

The teacher's greatest responsibility and opportunity is to present the study of the Christian way of living with such sympathy and breadth that the Christian religion is not merely accepted as one of the subjects of the curriculum, but revealed as the agent of fusion, the key to the understanding of life; as not only the integrator of all the work and world of school life, but also as the unifier of life in the world at large, the first interpreter of its real significance.

I. THE CHRISTIAN FAITH

Introductory

Christian faith is the human response to God's giving of Himself, and the Bible contains a record of that revelation of God upon which our knowledge of Him depends. The purpose of this course is to gather up the truths of which the Bible speaks and by which Christians live, so that boys and girls may perceive them clearly and understand at least the elements of Christianity as an approach to life. It is not intended that the course should be presented dogmatically, or in the form 'This is what a Christian must believe'. Sixth forms should work it out with their teacher in their own study and thought; the aim should be to arrive at some statement of faith, such as that suggested in the following pages, as a result of questioning, reading and discussion. In this course, headings are given under which the Christian faith may be studied and discussed, with indications of the type of conclusion which it should be the aim to reach. Sometimes a specific line of approach is suggested; sometimes the enlargement is left to the teacher. Many teachers may feel the necessity of recourse to a fuller treatment of the material here outlined than any syllabus can provide. Such aids to study and teaching will be found among the books listed on pp. 172–174. Reference to the great religions of the world other than Christianity, and to the relationship between religion, science and philosophy, will be almost inevitable in dealing with the central affirmations of the Christian faith, and the teacher should feel free to follow these leads provided the main pattern of the course is not thereby lost. The questions most likely to arise are those concerned with conduct. In this course they should be dealt with in connection with the particular beliefs with which they are most closely related, it being demonstrated that belief ultimately determines conduct.

Who are Christians?

We live in a country where freedom in religion is a cherished heritage, where Christian beliefs are respected and Christian standards of conduct are at least nominally admitted. When all has been said that can be said about the weakness of the Churches and the inconsistencies of men and women who profess to be Christians, it is unquestionable that the spirit and teaching of Christianity, though not always recognised, are still a real influence upon the life of the nation. Perplexing as the differences between denominations may be, there is among those who call themselves Christians a growing unity which makes it possible to say that they make up a body of people who build their lives upon certain definite experiences and beliefs, and upon certain definite views concerning specific events in history.

The Substance of the Faith

There have been many formulations of the faith, but apart from the earliest and simplest of all—'Jesus is Lord'—the Apostles' Creed is probably nearer in origin to the first century than any other, and is best calculated to assist the teacher to present the Christian faith. It may be summed up as follows:

Belief in
> God
> The Father
> Jesus Christ, His Son, Our Lord
> The Holy Spirit
> The Church
> The forgiveness of sins
> The life eternal

These eight points are adopted as the framework in the summary which follows.

The Meaning of Belief

There is all the difference between 'believing in' and 'believing that'. We can believe that a fact, like the Norman Conquest, really occurred and is not imagined, but this may make little or no practical difference to our daily thought and action. But if we believe in a principle or a person—in freedom, for example, or in God—we do not merely assent to a proposition: we are committed in heart and mind and soul, so that everything in our personalities and our relationships is affected by our belief. To believe *in* is to be impelled to action, whereas to believe *that* may leave us still detached and inactive. All action implies both kinds of belief. We cannot live as purposefully and effectively as we might if we do not try to think out clearly what are the facts to which we have to adjust ourselves, and why we regard them as facts. The Christian religion involves convictions regarding the meaning of historical facts. Faith and conduct, belief and action are thus inseparable for Christians, and that is why in the New Testament Christianity is described both as 'the Faith' and 'the Way'. It is in this sense that Christians believe in God, Father, Son and Holy Spirit. In so far as they are sincerely and actively Christians, this belief inspires and governs all that they think and do.

Belief in God

Christians are not the only people who believe in God. Jews and Mohammedans do so, and they think of God as personal, righteous and merciful. Hindus, Buddhists and Confucianists do not think of God in that way, but they too believe in an unseen and infinite Reality. Mankind has always been religious; the Christian is normal, not peculiar, in believing in God.

The Sense of Mystery

As soon as men think about life they are met by a mystery in it which moves them to wonder and awe. This sense of mystery may be, at its lowest, no more than superstitious fear born of ignorance: at its highest it leads to the recognition of supreme worth or value, and the impulse to serve it—that is to say, to worship. Man's impulse to unite himself in prayer, submission and worship to the Mystery which lies behind the world in which he lives, is normal. In a rational world a natural and normal impulse may reasonably be taken to point to the existence of an object fitted to satisfy it.

Mind and Design

In the higher religions the Object of Worship is conceived as the Power behind the universe, from which or from whom the life of nature and of man proceeds. Science explains the development of nature and of man without reference to God. On the other hand, the very possibility of science depends upon the fact that the character of the natural world is discoverable by the human mind. It is reasonable to suppose that the system which thus responds to mind is itself the work of mind; and in that case, of a Mind which is infinite and universal, since, if it has made the world, it cannot be entirely contained in the world. But a Mind beyond the things that are seen and temporal, is (in part) what we mean by God, and is a worthy object of worship. Whether or not religion arose historically out of the desire to explain a mysterious universe, belief in God does satisfy the desire to give to ourselves some account of the meaning of the world in which we live, and of ourselves as part of the world.

The Moral Sense

Man has a sense of right and wrong. People may differ widely in their judgments of what is right and what is wrong in particular. But all agree that there are actions that are right and actions that are wrong, and that we 'ought' to do right. This 'ought' is felt as a supreme obligation, and conscience acknowledges its authority. For the individual this 'ought' may in part be the good of his community, but can never be identified with it: the 'ought' to which allegiance is ultimately due is above and beyond a man's duty to his group. In the higher religions, the Object of Worship is conceived as this authority, which conscience recognises.

Religion a Normal Activity

Religion, then, is normal to humanity. Man is 'incurably religious'. Of this we have overwhelming evidence in primitive beliefs, in the great world religions, and even in 'substitutes' for religion both in the ancient and modern world, such as the cult of the Emperor or the State, dictator worship or a creed of race supremacy. As he considers nature, history and his own conscious life, man desires an explanation of his experience, and at the same time there is, deep within him, the desire to worship. Even religions which began, like Buddhism, without belief in a personal God, have ended by deifying their founders, or if, like Hinduism, they are rooted in pantheism, they have created mythical or legendary figures of the gods, like those in the *Bhagavad-gita*.

The Nature of the Christian's God

This universal need is met in Hebrew religion by a belief in a personal God, holy, righteous and merciful. In the light of His existence, His character and His purpose the Jews explained the existence of the world and of the human race, the course of history and the hope of a better world; men were made that they might have personal relationship with God; He required men to do justly, to love mercy and to walk humbly with Him. The Hebrew prophets were inspired to see the hand of God in history and to call their contemporaries to new standards in worship and conduct; their insight was such as no other religious teachers before Christ had ever possessed.

They constitute one of the few groups of men who decisively altered history in any intimate sense. Most spectacular upheavals of history merely replace one set of individuals by another analogous set; so that history is mostly a barren change of names. But the Hebrew prophets really produced a decisive qualitative alteration, and what is still more rare, a change for the better. (WHITEHEAD.)

The Christian belief in God is based upon the revelation of God recorded in the New Testament, completing and fulfilling that of the Old Testament. It is far more than a mere development of 'natural religion' or a refinement of Judaism. What Christianity means by 'God' can be understood only when all that is set forth in the following paragraphs has been grasped. To know God as Father, to see the grace and truth of God in Jesus Christ, to experience the guidance and power of God active in the Holy Spirit, imparts to our lives a meaning and a quality which do not result from merely believing *that* He exists. The Christian religion is essentially belief *in* God, and the bringing of our *whole lives* into relation with Him as He has been revealed to us.

Belief in God the Father, Maker of Heaven and Earth

In Judaism and Christianity God is worshipped and believed in not as a mere force or as bare Reality, but as the personal Creator and Sustainer of the Universe. The earliest religious traditions of the Hebrews present God as real and personal, creating and controlling all things—in contrast with Babylonian and other mythical accounts of the origin of the universe. The insistence that God created and that He governs is expressed in thought-forms which do not agree with those of twentieth-century science, but modern scientific theories do not necessarily conflict with the Biblical belief in the creative and directing activity of a living God.[1] But His purpose and character, as the Prophets perceived, are more important than His power. Even in the Old Testament God is depicted as using His power only within the limits He has set Himself, having given Man free-will to choose evil and bring upon himself the consequent suffering (the story of the Fall). God wishes men to partake of His character, to follow His plan. Refusal to do so is wrong-doing and damages relationship with Him. But while God cannot be untrue to Himself by regarding wrong-doing as anything but what it is, His desire is that men who have done wrong should sincerely repent and turn to Him with faith that He will forgive. 'The Lord is gracious and full of compassion, slow to anger and of great mercy.' It is thus that He is set forth in those parts of the Old Testament which contain, through Hebrew religious insight, the fullest revelation of God to man before the coming of Jesus. (The mature prophetic conception of God may be compared both with the naïve and patently inadequate ideas about Him held by the early Hebrews as well as with those found in other religions.)

The conception of God as Father is found in the Old Testament, but only rarely. It is not fully developed there, and does not supplant the thought of God as Almighty Creator and Ruler; but it adds to it the important idea of One who enters into personal relations with His people, and so prepares the way for the full revelation of Divine Fatherhood in the New Testament.

[1] Chapters II and III of J. W. Hunkin's *Is it Reasonable to Believe?* are helpful here.

Jesus gave a new meaning to the description of God as Father. This meaning arose from His own experience of a relationship to God—of knowledge, love and obedience—for which Sonship was the only fitting expression. 'My Father and your Father'; the parable of the prodigal son; 'How much more shall your Father in heaven give good things to those that ask Him'; the Lord's Prayer; Jesus' own prayers, especially in Gethsemane; the cry 'Father, into thy hands...'; 'the true worshippers shall worship the Father in spirit and in truth'; 'ye shall be perfect as your Father in heaven is perfect'. A 'brotherhood of man' based upon the fact of a common humanity is different from a brotherhood derived from a common sonship of God (St Matthew v. 44-45). The two great commands of Jesus—love of God and love of neighbour.

Belief in Jesus Christ, His Son, Our Lord

In the Old Testament the presence and power of God are recognised in a special way in the history of a chosen people. 'I am the Lord thy God, which brought thee up out of the land of Egypt' expresses the starting point of the religion of the children of Israel. They always felt aware that they had been called, as a people, to be God's people; they were not always faithful to that calling. They passed through great sufferings, defeat, enslavement, exile. Other peoples have been through such experiences; but this people learned, through the prophets, that the strange adventures of their history were no mere accidents, but lay under the providence of God. Through these adventures He was leading them to a fuller knowledge of Himself, and teaching them what it meant to be His people. Thus history became a revelation of God. But it was never a complete revelation. There would yet come (so they believed) a day when finally God would make Himself known. For many this belief took shape in the expectation of a mysterious figure—the 'Messiah', as they called Him (God's 'Anointed', or accredited representative) whom God would raise up in time to come to accomplish His purpose. The Old Testament leaves us with this expectation and the New Testament declares it to have been fulfilled in Jesus Christ; God's revelation was completed.

The life of Jesus was a fact in history. This is the starting point of believing *that*, with all that follows for believing *in*. Compare Christianity both with those religions (Hinduism, Confucianism) which do not profess to depend upon historical fact, and with those which have a historical core (Judaism, Buddhism, Islam) yet do not rest upon belief that the Son of God 'for us men and for our salvation...was made man'. The gospel of St Mark begins with the Baptism ('Thou art my beloved Son') and shows what men who lived with Him on the earth found in Jesus.

Redemption

The Crucifixion of Jesus disclosed, in the first place, the extent of the perversion in human nature. There were indeed ideals and good intentions on all sides. Civilised government, organised religion and patriotism are not bad things in themselves. Pilate might have passed for a competent administrator, Caiaphas for a prudent ecclesiastical statesman, the Zealots for high-souled patriots, and the Pharisees for men of genuine if narrow piety, if they had not been confronted with Jesus; but the perverse following of their own aims compelled them to put Him out of the way. Secondly, the Crucifixion revealed the spirit in which Jesus faced the situation. His whole career was shaped by absolute obedience to the will of God, an obedience not to be deflected by any consideration of consequences. Faced with powerful opposition, He would not compromise the truth of God, nor would He betray the love of God for men by the use of force. He chose the only alternative; He accepted for Himself, and drew upon His own person, the evil consequences of the wrong attitudes of others. All wrong-doing entails suffering on somebody, not necessarily on the guilty. If the innocent accepts the suffering willingly in the place of the wrong-doer, it can call back, as it were, the evil consequences of the wrong-doing; it has redemptive value instead of being mere disaster. The author of Isaiah liii had seen that; and there is good reason to believe that Jesus found in that Scripture an indication of the will of God for Him, and so went to His death as 'a ransom for many' (St Mark x. 45).

The Resurrection

For the disciples the Crucifixion was a severe trial of their faith. They had not only lost their Master; all that they had hoped and trusted in had been shattered. God, it appeared, had failed to save His Servant from His fate. The Resurrection was not simply their recovery of a lost friend; it was their recovery of faith in the purpose and power of God revealed in Jesus of Nazareth.

The Divinity of Christ

It is this course of events, thus understood in experience, that the New Testament writers set out to interpret, and their interpretation is the basis of Christian belief. The title 'Messiah' or 'Christ' indicates their belief in His divine mission to change the world; that of 'Lord' the absolute loyalty they owed to Him, as to God Himself; that of 'Saviour' the deliverance from sin and evil which He had brought them. ('Lord' and 'Saviour' are both divine titles in the Old Testament.) From Jesus Himself they had learned to call Him 'Son of God'. Finally they recognised in Him the 'Wisdom' or 'Word' of God incarnate, and thereby their understanding of Him was brought within the field of philosophical thought.

Thus the Christian faith is that Jesus is truly God and truly man. The divine and the human are united in Him in a way that we cannot understand. The Apostles' Creed expresses the fact in the two clauses 'conceived by the Holy Ghost, born of the Virgin Mary'. These clauses have received diverse interpretations.[1] But all are agreed that the Incarnation is a fact, the central fact of Christianity. 'God was in Him' as God has been in no other man. As with the Incarnation, so with the Resurrection and Ascension. 'He came forth from God and goeth unto God' (St John xiii. 3). Moreover, the Christian belief is that in the end all men will be confronted with God as He is revealed in Christ; the Apostles' Creed expresses this in the clause 'He shall come...'.

---

[1] The differences between representative thinkers in the Church of England are clearly stated in *Doctrine in the Church of England*, issued by the Archbishops' Commission.

God revealed in Suffering

Because their experience of revelation and redemption turned upon His death, as interpreted by His resurrection, the New Testament writers made the Cross central to their whole new understanding of God. They set forth the death of Christ as the culmination of a life of perfect obedience to God; as a clear condemnation of the wrong-doing responsible, and with it, of all sin and wrong-doing; as the greatest example of God's love to erring men; and thus, as the fulfilment of God's purpose in sending His Son to kindle in human hearts a responsive love and faith towards Him.

'The good news of Christianity is that suffering is itself divine. It is not foreign to the experience of God Himself. "In all their affliction He was afflicted." "Surely He hath borne our griefs and carried our sorrow...". The divine suffering is not an episode, but a revelation. It is the necessary form which divine love takes, when it is brought into contact with evil. To overcome evil with good means to suffer unjustly and willingly.' (INGE.)

Belief in the Holy Spirit

What do we mean by 'the spirit of a man that is in him'? We think of 'spirit' in terms of life, energy, the qualities that make a man what he is and are expressed in character and action. Those who lived with Jesus during His ministry saw and felt in Him the Spirit of God; 'God anointed Him with the Holy Ghost and with power' (Peter, Acts x. 38); 'God was in Christ' (Paul, II Corinthians v. 19). The gospel-writers expressed this feeling through the symbolism of the Spirit 'descending and resting' upon Him.

Even before Pentecost there was in Jerusalem a group of men and women held together in a spiritual unity by a common allegiance to the Risen Christ and by a common expectation of His return. At Pentecost, when that expectation was in part fulfilled by the coming of the Holy Spirit, this sense of one-ness in Christ was confirmed, and the community became conscious of itself as the body of people dwelt in by the Spirit of Christ, and inspired by Him to increasing knowledge and understanding of the 'message about Christ'. They were now experiencing God in yet a new way, not only as Father and Son, but as indwelling, transforming Spirit, bringing power to overcome sin, light upon the Way of Life, and strength to achieve what was impossible before.

After the Resurrection and Pentecost men and women who 'sanctified in their hearts Christ Jesus as Lord' found a new courage, love and insight. They ascribed this to the Spirit they had seen in Jesus and which they recognised must be God. Paul's phrases are not merely variations, but attempts to express the truth from many angles—'the Spirit of Christ', 'the Spirit of God', 'the grace of the Lord Jesus Christ and the love of God, and the fellowship of the Holy Spirit'. The coming of the Holy Spirit to men and women who responded to the teaching of Jesus marks the channel by which a new quality of life is made available to man.

Belief in the Church

The early Hebrews believed that a man was related to God because he was a member of the people with whom God had made a covenant. Within this corporate religion there arose a sense of individual responsibility towards God, especially proclaimed by Jeremiah and Ezekiel, although the idea of personal relationship with God began to be realised before them. Jesus set a higher value than ever upon the individual, but at the same time insisted that the children of God are a family, a community.

As Israel was made the people of God by a covenant, so the new covenant of which Jesus spoke at the Last Supper meant a new Israel, a people of God called to worship, service and the winning of all men to the way of God (St Luke xxii. 25–29; St Matthew xxviii. 18–20).

The worship and witness of the Early Church are described in Acts, from which and from the Epistles we get pictures of various local churches, at Jerusalem, Antioch, Corinth, Ephesus; 'Salute the church that is in their house' (Colossians iv. 15, and R.V. margin).

The Christian community has passed the message on for some sixty generations without a break; although the Church has in the course of history become disunited, what is held in common is still more important than the points of difference, which have generally arisen from a one-sided emphasis laid upon some neglected truth. Membership in the 'Body of Christ' is not possible in isolation but must be completed through the sharing of Christian witness and experience with others; the individual both receives from, and contributes to, the community.

The Forgiveness of Sins

Sins arise from what we do, sinfulness from what we are. We are continually being faced with moral decisions, small and great; it is what we are, before the moment of decision comes, that chiefly determines what we do. Hence Jesus' emphasis on motive and choice. The Ten Commandments of the Old Testament are mostly concerned with actions; the two great commandments of Jesus are concerned with dispositions and attitudes. He reversed conventional ideas about right and wrong, both in His teaching (the rich young ruler) and in His own dealings with social and national outcasts (Zacchaeus, Levi, the woman in the Pharisee's house, the woman of Samaria, the Syrophenician woman).

Our sense of right and wrong is illuminated by the life and teaching of Jesus. Sin is not an offence against a code, with a legal penalty attached: sins are things done, which cannot be undone, but they arise from a wrong attitude to God, and this attitude can be changed; that is why the sinner is called to repentance. Jesus never condoned a sin, but he was always prepared to forgive a repentant sinner. Sin is always against God, because it is always a rejection of God's will for us as members of His family; it is often against our fellow-men as well. It is worst when it is against those who go on loving and believing in us when they are hurt by what we do and are. The people who opposed Jesus and brought Him to His death sinned against Him and against God in Him. The Cross is seen as the supreme evidence of the depth of God's love for man. 'Greater love hath no man than this, that a man lay down his life for his friends.' The death of Jesus was the inevitable result of His opposition to the sinful state, the wrong attitude of those around Him; but He faced it knowingly and willingly, as the only effective way, God's way, in which this wrong attitude could be overcome. Jesus took upon himself the role of the Suffering Servant of Isaiah liii. Jesus' own example of forgiveness is seen in his attitude to Peter, following his denial, 'Lovest thou me?' The aim of forgiveness is to restore and increase fellowship. 'Forgive us our trespasses, as we also forgive them that trespass against us.' Atonement represents reconciliation, not of God to men, but of men to God. Forgiveness releases the motive power to live a new life, no longer controlled by the old wrong attitudes.

Belief in Eternal Life

Christianity took over the conviction, slowly gaining ground during the later Old Testament period and afterwards, that the fellowship with God which may be established here upon earth is not destroyed by death.

Jesus taught that God is not the God of the dead, but of the living (St Matthew xxii. 32); the life to come is not subject to the conditions of this life (St Matthew xxii. 30). The Resurrection confirmed Jesus' teaching which is elaborated especially in the Fourth Gospel (St John xiv. 3; xi. 25; xiv. 19; iii. 16). Life Eternal is not merely a matter of living after death, but life of a new quality, fully demonstrated in Jesus and made possible now for us through Him; it is a relationship with God which is independent of time. It springs from knowledge of God—'This is life eternal, that they should know thee, the only true God, and him whom thou didst send, even Jesus Christ' (St John xvii. 3). It is also experienced in sharing the life and love of God as this comes to men in Jesus Christ (St John v. 26, 39–40; xvii. 21–26). It follows then that for Christians death is not the end of everything, it is just a very important change. It is not merely that a part of us will go on after death, but that we ourselves will go on, and that the new life we lead after the death of our bodies is one of new spiritual growth. Many reasons have been urged for belief in immortality. But for Christians the ultimate conviction comes from their belief in the nature of God revealed in Jesus: 'Who through him are believers in God, which raised him from the dead and gave him glory; so that your faith and hope might be in God.'

Note. In taking the foregoing course many teachers will wish to consult a fuller treatment of the material outlined. There are a number of short but good books written from varying points of view, any or all of which the teacher will find useful to possess. Among them may be mentioned J. W. Hunkin's *Is It Reasonable to Believe?*[1] and J. G. Riddell's *What We Believe.*[2] Others are referred to in the Book List. Whatever method of teaching is adopted, questions and discussions will in many cases arise spontaneously. Such books as *Asking them Questions*[3] show in what form the problems of faith present themselves to boys and girls, and are a useful reminder of the necessity of relating formal and even Biblical statements of Christian truth to the experience, the mental capacity and the language of boys and girls.

II. THE BIBLE AND CHRISTIAN TEACHING

The purpose of this course is to make members of a sixth form aware that:

(1) There is an indispensable inheritance of teaching concerning God and Man contained in the Bible which is relevant to-day. If this is accepted Christianity is the inescapable conclusion, which makes a challenge not lightly to be dismissed.

(2) Its study demands as full intellectual effort, both in truth-seeking and accurate learning, as any other subject.

(3) Ultimately it must call for personal decision, that is, belief or disbelief. Belief is not vague opinion but self-committal in the face of certain reasonable evidence. Disbelief is a positive attitude also; it must somehow account for the evidence in another way.

The course may be covered in outline in a year, or enlarged at different stages to cover two years or more. It can also be made adaptable to different sixth form groups according to various needs and levels in different schools, but it assumes the studies of previous years in the *Cambridgeshire Syllabus*, whilst allowing for the fact that, even with the best teaching, what is learnt in earlier years is not always retained.

[1] Hodder and Stoughton's Westminster Books, 1935.
[2] Church of Scotland Committee on Publications, 1938.
[3] Edited by R. Selby Wright, two series, 1936 and 1938, Oxford University Press.

A suggested outline is given which each teacher will develop for himself. It may help to meet the perennial problem of 'letting them raise questions' as opposed to 'getting on with the course and seeing that they know something', if Bible passages to be read are put up for a term, or week by week, in advance. Those giving plenty of time to their Scripture will be able to use commentaries and read round the subject. (It will conduce to sound work if *The Clarendon Bible Commentaries* are continuously available.) For those whose time is limited, some definite weekly study of the Bible itself should be secured as the minimum, or else the general nature of the course may result in very superficial work. Short books such as C. H. Dodd's *The Bible To-day* and H. Balmforth's *The Christian Religion* could profitably be read by all pupils during the course.

Part I. History

The Bible

From the beginning it should not be forgotten that there are two 'orders' in both Old Testament and New Testament.

(1) That in which they were written, which is important for understanding the growth of the literature and the development of ideas.

(2) That in which they were bound up, which shows us the purpose of those who gave us the Bible in its present form. It is this second order which presents to us the complete picture of creation, Man's sin and the long history of God's redemptive activity.

It should also be remembered that:

(1) *The Old Testament* as a whole is a product of the teaching of the prophets and the work of the priests and others after the Return from Babylon.

(2) The literature which comes *between the Old and the New Testaments* is important for the developments which took place, and which must be grasped for the proper understanding of the New Testament. It illustrates, as it were, the stage upon which the drama of the New Testament was acted.

(3) *The New Testament* represents the growth of a new faith and the beginning of its formulation. Its central events are seen in the light of their direct results and of reflection upon them, but from a point still sufficiently close to the events to embody also the record of first-hand experience.

The Bible's Frontispiece (Genesis i–iii)

Taking the Bible in its present order we begin with answers, in story form, to fundamental questions as to the origin of the world, of man, and of sin. Some of the stories are based on the myths that were recited when rituals were performed; some of them arise from ancient folk-lore, and others embody earliest attempts at science and philosophy. God is shown as the Creator, and Man as made 'in His image' but fallen short of goodness through misuse of the freedom inherent in this likeness, thus impairing his friendship with God through disobedience to His purpose and expressed will.

The rest of the Old Testament is the story of the gradual revelation of God to men, culminating in the New Testament gospel 'God was in Christ reconciling the world unto Himself' (II Corinthians v. 19).

The Gradual Revelation of God in the Old Testament

(The following section should be illustrated by Biblical references, and in some cases, by documentary comparisons; help may be obtained in the selection of these from such a book as W. O. E. Oesterley and T. H. Robinson's *An Introduction to the Books of the Old Testament*.)

The final editors of the Old Testament looked back to God's choice of Abraham and his descendants as the 'peculiar people' through whom he was to reveal Himself (in contrast to the deities of the seasonal and agricultural religions common at the time in the Near East).

God is next portrayed in 'the Law' as showing His will, for the whole life of the people, secular as well as religious.

The writers of the historical books show God as active in the life of the nation, rewarding and punishing.

Through the prophets God revealed Himself as concerned with human behaviour. The individual experiences and main contributions of the prophets should be reviewed, with a summing up at each stage of ideas reached concerning (i) the nature of God, (ii) God's ways with men.

Reference should be made to:

(1) The prophets and the community, and the idea of 'The Remnant'.
(2) The individual and the community, with emphasis upon 'The New Covenant'.
(3) Key passages in Isaiah xl—lv.

In the devotional beauty of the Psalms God is seen as the object of Man's worship.

The Forward Look

The Old Testament is characterised by an expectation of God's special intervention, a belief which grew stronger as the actual conditions of the Jews became worse. Each prophet spoke to his own time about the religious questions and material problems of his day, but underlying some of their utterances were truths concerning the nature and purpose of God which are timeless. As we look back we can see, in the light of the New Testament, a deeper meaning in their words, and a fulfilment in the life and teaching of Jesus.

The Kingdom of God

The prophetic teaching had centred in the ideal of a people obedient to the rule of a righteous God. But post-prophetic Judaism left vague the time and manner in which the Kingdom of God was to be realised, and there were many differing ideas about it; there is a strong emphasis in the Old Testament in its present form on the idealised figure of David and his royal line (Isaiah xi. 1) and a righteous king (Zechariah ix. 9, cf. St Mark xi. 10); the prophets had pictured a 'Day of the Lord' (Malachi iii. 1–3) to express the idea of God's intervention and His holiness; later this is seen as the day of the Son of Man (Daniel vii. 13); this is equated with the day when the 'saints of the most High' shall receive the Kingdom (Daniel vii. 18) and the kingly rule of God shall become effective over the whole world (Daniel vii. 27).

The New Testament opens with the proclamation of the Kingdom.

The world to which the Saviour came

(1) Summary of Jewish national history from the Return; the quarrel with the Greek authorities; the Maccabees, the worldly success under John Hyrcanus, the failure under Alexander Jannaeus, the coming of the Romans.

It should be shown:

(a) How various groups were produced, e.g. Sadducees, Pharisees, Essenes, Zealots, the Jews of the Dispersion.
(b) How religious life and thought developed, illustrated in the Temple, the synagogues, the Law, the attraction of Hellenism, the realisation that an earthly kingdom was impossible, the growth of the 'other world' idea, apocalyptic expectations.

(2) A sense of urgency and tension characterised a time when deep and vital questions were being asked but not answered. Political events and the pressure of Hellenism had given rise to a searching re-examination of Judaism among the Jews themselves.

If the Jews were God's Chosen People, why had he allowed them to suffer eclipse? (The attitude of disillusion can be seen in Ecclesiastes.)

If Israel's God is the only God, can His kingdom be limited to Israel? Nationalism and universalism (Isaiah xl–lv; Jonah).

If God's rule is a righteous rule, why do the righteous suffer? Can a righteous God allow the righteous to perish? Divine justice and the destiny of the individual (the main issue of Job, taken briefly; Psalm lxxiii). The idea of the Suffering Servant lay dormant, as it were, until the time of Jesus (Isaiah liii). Who could say what righteousness really was or how it was attained? (The Book of Wisdom still leaves the problem unanswered.)

If the 'sacrifices of God are a broken spirit...', what is the place of the Temple ritual? (Compare the different attitude in *v.* 19 of Psalm li to that of the rest of the Psalm.)

If God has given over this world to the dominion of evil, where and when shall His kingdom be realised? Pessimism and 'other-worldliness'. (Daniel and Apocalyptists.)

Daily events were charged with significance for the Jews, believing as they did in one Holy God who would save His people. This conscious feeling of 'the necessity of Christ' is met by John the Baptist's announcement. The questions put to the Baptist, together with the answers he gave and the novel symbolism he used to convey his message, give a picture of a people full of seeking expectancy. This is further illustrated by Paul's state of mind before his conversion, as expressed in his persecuting violence, and as described by himself in Romans vii.

The Proclamation. *'This is that which hath been spoken'*

The life and death of Jesus made comparatively small stir at the time; for the majority, the tension and waiting remained. Later events caused that life and death to be intimately recalled, recorded and studied.

What happened on the day of Pentecost? What was the Good News, which supplied the answers so eagerly awaited? (Summarise the first Christian preaching and its significance; Peter's speech, Acts ii. 14–39.) Emergence of the Christian community as 'the New Israel of God', characterised by 'a new kind of community life exhibiting the marks of inward spiritual power in its freedom, unity and constructive energy' (C. H. Dodd, *The Bible To-day*). The achievements of the early Christians illustrate this.

Part II. The Teaching of Jesus and the Christian Faith

Historical examination of the Bible leads on to a more detailed study of Jesus Christ, His life and teaching, and the faith of His followers.

A. The Life and Teaching of Jesus

(1) A quick review of the life of Jesus, based on St Mark's Gospel; the awakening and unfolding of His purpose revealed through the outstanding events of His baptism; His temptation; the proclamation of the Kingdom; Peter's confession of faith; the transfiguration; 'setting His face' to go to Jerusalem; Gethsemane; the climax. The drama should be carried on to Acts ii, so that the undeniable change wrought in men, rather than merely the empty tomb, is the final note.

(2) A review of Jesus' teaching in the light of its setting. (Useful reference can be made to books such as C. H. Dodd's *Parables of the Kingdom*, O. C. Quick's *Realism of Christ's Parables*, A. D. Lindsay's *The Moral Teaching of Jesus*, E. F. Scott's *The Ethical Teaching of Jesus*.) The Sermon on the Mount will raise the question of conduct and absolute standards. Here will be an opportunity to develop the meaning of Christian Love. 'God is Love'—but what kind of Love? Members of a sixth form want to raise practical questions, but constantly do so from the end where something has gone wrong, because they have no ideal before them; they will discuss divorce rather than marriage, gambling rather than earning, or approach questions from an angle of 'social welfare'. While interest in these questions may often be the starting point, it is important eventually to get behind them and consider the practical application of Christianity to the life of the individual and society. It is from questions of conduct, from consideration of man's failures and man's need, that the 16–18 age will best come to a clear summing-up of the Christian faith.

(3) *St John's Gospel*

No sixth form boy or girl should leave school without some knowledge of the Fourth Gospel. Discussion on it should include:

(a) A frank recognition of the problems raised by its discrepancies in history from the synoptic gospels.

(b) Its great importance as presenting eternal and universal truths through the incidents which it relates.

B. *The History, Faith and Worship of the Christian Church*

(1) *The Community:*

(a) *History*

The founding of the Church; the Jewish antecedents of the Church—the Chosen People; the Remnant, Jesus as 'the Bridge', the Apostles; the old Covenant and the New Covenant; brief reference to the development of the Church over 1900 years; compare the early church as depicted in the New Testament with a young overseas church.

(b) Christian Fellowship

What is the Church? Its four characteristics described in Acts ii. 42. The unity of the Church is dependent from the beginning upon the Fellowship created, maintained and developed by the common sharing in the outpouring of the Holy Spirit (Acts ii). In this Fellowship Christ is present to express the love of God in every need of man (I Corinthians xii and Ephesians i–iv). There is a great deal of teaching in the New Testament about corporate as well as about personal religion, and teachers may find it convenient to make use of the references set out in the Course on 'Personal and Corporate Religion' on pp. 94–98. The New Testament and the history of the Church contain constant illustrations of God's love for man which can and should be rendered within and through the Fellowship in the name of Christ.

(c) Belief

There is a danger at this stage in using theological phrases and even credal summaries before the beliefs have been seen in terms of human experience; e.g. there must be some appreciation of a sense of wrong-doing leading to discomfort, to acknowledgment, to release and renewal, before this progression can be spoken of in terms of 'sin', 'confession', 'redemption' and 'grace'. The Church's belief was that it possessed 'through' and 'in' Jesus Christ a real deliverance from all the evil of the world. This deliverance meant a new relationship to God, that of sons to a Father. It was 'through' Jesus because He had shown in Himself the full meaning of sonship to God, victory by self-sacrifice over the worst that the world could do. But it was also 'in' Jesus because the new sense of sonship came by way of a spiritual and personal union with the living Christ. The belief was not at first formulated in any creed, but it expresses itself in certain classic statements of the New Testament: Galatians i. 3–4; Romans v. 1–11; John iii. 16–19; II Corinthians v. 18–19; Romans viii (especially 12–17, 28–29); II Corinthians xiii. 14. These are expressions or reflections of Christian *experience*. The consequence of that experience was a new understanding of the nature of God Himself, implicit in the New Testament statements, but not drawn out into a formal doctrine until much later. The ancient Jewish faith in *One* God was never abandoned, but it came to be seen that *within* the Divine Unity there are three 'personal' activities or realities: God as the unseen source of all good, the Father; God as made visible in His own likeness, the Son; God as reproducing that likeness in the fellowship of Christian believers, the Spirit (cf. John xvii. 20–26).

(d) Worship

The idea and value of corporate worship inherent in the Jewish Church was endorsed and revalued by our Lord in His example and teaching. The prayer which He commended to His followers is the prayer of a community (St Matthew vi. 9–13; *our, us*). Reference has already been made to the essential character of the Church as described in Acts ii. 42, where direct allusion is made to corporate prayer. This was so regular a practice in the early Church that we find it as the assumed activity of the Christian Fellowship (Acts xii. 5). The gathering together for 'the breaking of bread and the prayers' (Acts ii. 42; xx. 7; I Corinthians xi. 17–34).

Note. The references in the section on Prayer in the Junior section on pp. 46–48 may be found useful at this point, as well as H. E. Fosdick's *The Meaning of Prayer*. For the meaning of Worship and Fellowship a helpful book is *How Christians Worship*, a set of broadcasts on ancient and modern ways of worship in the different churches; and reference may be made to the note on 'School Worship' on p. 12.

(2) The Individual

The need for a new birth (St John iii. 3; II Corinthians v. 17), a venture of faith; the Christian makes no claim to be better than others, but recognises his need and accepts certain definite obligations. Why go to church? What is a 'Christian' life?

(3) Eternal Life

'This is life eternal, that they might know thee' (literally 'that they might come to know thee') 'the only true God, and Jesus Christ, whom thou hast sent.' (St John xvii. 3.)

(a) Faith

To live in the light of Christ, to forget self and see the world as God's world, is to have a *kind* of life which rises above the restlessness of change. The Christian here and now can enter into this new quality of life.

(*b*) *Hope*

This experience of eternal life releases us from the fear of death; and at the same time assures us that death can have no power to destroy it.

(*c*) *Love*

This experience is the knowledge of God who is Love, and who will not suffer us to be separated from Him or from those in whose love we learnt to know His.

III. SPECIFIC BOOKS AS SEPARATE COURSES

It has been felt that an endeavour to provide a syllabus for the sixth form could not be considered complete without some reference to the form use of a book written by a well-qualified author. Such a book can either be on a strictly scriptural theme or upon some other subject of definitely religious associations. A selection of such books as have already proved of value in this way will be found on p. 133. Every sixth form teacher will be able to add to the list.

The advantages of such a course, as a supplement to courses directly based on books of the Bible, are not confined to the intrinsic merit of the book concerned; for they lie not only in the immediate burden of enlightenment there given, but also in the provocation of useful argument and discussion on related problems and perplexities already existing in pupils' minds. The possession of a copy of the book by each pupil, moreover, meets that difficulty with which teachers are so often confronted and which they strive to meet by the issue of synopses and summaries— the pupils' need for a background of material both for preparation and for constant casual reference. The type of book chosen for such a course will always involve the Bible, directly and indirectly; but the Bible at large is a most discouraging wilderness in which to search for the corroboration of some fact or quotation vaguely remembered from an earlier lesson. Even if the subject is a specific book of the Bible and a commentary is in use, it is often difficult to find one suitable for school purposes, since the majority deal overmuch in notes on abstruse points and tend to obscure the contours of the wood in their attention to individual trees. As more and more men on the ground seek to write their own commentaries, or follow the block-method and wide sweep of such a book as J. A. Findlay's *Acts of the Apostles* this situation will improve.

As has been indicated, however, there is another approach to the teaching of religious knowledge than the direct exposition of scripture, with its 'leads' out into the everyday world of which boys and girls are intimately aware. This other approach starts from the outside and works inwards; it begins at the periphery of life, with its science and philosophy, its ethics of daily life as generally lived, its popular psychology, its problems, personal, social, national and international, which arouse a varying but immediate interest in the minds of pupils; it then bends inwards from this outer world, and turns to the Bible and the gospel of salvation provided by God in Christ for this world's desperate need. Here are the answers, and here is the divine solution; but before the answers and solutions are given, the problems and the questions should be firmly compassed and realised.

This is where the use of a carefully chosen book offers a basis for adventuring. It combines the merit of starting from where the pupil is with the advantage of providing the requisite background for reference and study. The experienced teacher knows the need for constant repetition and recapitulation. In embarking upon a course, the teacher is, or should be, well aware of his objective, the general route towards it, and the manifold detail involved on the way. Not so the pupil, who constantly feels the need for confirmation of hazy memories of details once described, for backward reference to the road already travelled, and for some indication of the direction of the way yet to be traversed. Herein lies the usefulness of a book in the hands of the pupil.

The method is open to abuse. Employed by a lazy teacher it may be regarded as a convenient device for absolving him from the careful preparation of lessons. But in the hands of a con-scientious teacher, who knows just why he is using a particular book and has his own critical contribution to add, the method is of proven value. Any book to be used in this way must be carefully selected for its quality to act as a key to life and outlook in the twentieth century; in addition to providing the framework which gives coherence to the course, it must have the capacity to provoke a variety of questions. The apt handling of these questions and the indication of what is implied by the application of the Gospel message to them will be the justification for choosing a particular book, and for using a method which begins with the world we know in order to throw us back upon the divine answer to that world's needs; the answer contained in the timeless pages of the Bible, the supreme solution proclaimed by the New Testament.

It frequently happens that questions for discussion arise naturally, spontaneously asked by members of the form. These are often couched in what, to a mature mind, may appear to be a naïve form, but they disclose the real difficulties and sincere searchings of older adolescents. Every sixth form teacher allowing free discussion in his class will be familiar with the type of question. A number have been collected in *Asking Them Questions*[1] with answers written by different authorities. These answers may not always be in the form which a particular teacher would choose, but in most cases they will be found helpful. Many of these questions may arise out of one piece of teaching or another and be dealt with as they occur, but when a set scheme of teaching is being followed, it may act as a refreshing change to set aside a period or two every now and again to the method employed in these books.

The following short list of books is a sample of those which have been found valuable when used in this way. Teachers will know many others which can be similarly used, and future publications will doubtless extend the range of choice.

SAYERS, D. *The Man Born to be King*. Gollancz, 1947.

SAYERS, D. *Creed or Chaos*. Methuen, 1947.

SKINNER, C. *The Gospel of the Lord Jesus*. University of London Press, 1937.

WHALE, J. S. *Facing the Facts*. Hodder and Stoughton, 1940.

LEWIS, C. S. *Broadcast Addresses*. Centenary Press, 1942.

LEWIS, C. S. *Christian Behaviour*. Bles, 1943.

LEWIS, C. S. *Beyond Personality*. Bles, 1944.

LINDSAY, A. D. *The Two Moralities*. Eyre and Spottiswoode, 1940.

BARRY, F. R. *Christianity and Psychology*. S.C.M., 1923.

REID, J. *Why Be Good?* Hodder and Stoughton, 1935.

[1] Edited by R. Selby Wright, two series, 1936 and 1938, Oxford University Press.

IV. ALTERNATIVE COURSES

After the sixth form has pursued some comprehensive study of the Bible or the Christian faith, many teachers may wish to get away from the traditional type of course, which is essentially a course in history, to one in which contemporary religious ideas are more prominent. It may be done, as has already been suggested, by the use of a specific book, or by the method of seeking the answers to certain questions. Some teachers may prefer to attempt this approach by yet other means. One may be able to follow through a course showing the position and influence of Christianity in the world to-day, in which may be included, or which may lead to, some study of comparative religion. Another may find it easier to show the relevance of Christianity for to-day by tracing out its history and development from the first to the twentieth century. With a sixth form which has some knowledge of textual criticism or the evaluation of historical documents, an examination may be made of the manuscripts on whose authority the New Testament rests. A study can be made of individual gospels, in the course of which something of their literary structure as revealed by criticism can be made apparent. Obviously, however, that is only a small part of the teacher's task when he is teaching a gospel. By imaginative treatment of the text he will be introducing his pupils to the basic ideas of Christian ethics and Christian theology. Other possibilities include a course on the development of the idea of God, from the tribal god of some Old Testament passages to the God of the prophets, the Wisdom literature and the Stoics, to the God of St Paul, the first three Gospels and the Fourth Gospel; a course on St Paul's life and letters, or some study of the Epistles; a course on the development of early Christianity; or one on materialism and the life of the spirit, perhaps using the *Phaedo* of Plato as a text-book.[1]

It is not easy to frame a course in which contemporary religious ideas are given reality and come alive; but the good teacher will find a means of doing it, and some of the foregoing suggestions may be helpful.

[1] In connection with these suggestions, it may be found useful to consult the Book List at the end of the Syllabus.

NOTES

CLASSES IN THE SMALL SCHOOL

Infants

In schools where all children from 5 to 7 are taught in one class, the topics suggested for the years 5 and 6 must be thought of as a two-year programme of Scripture teaching. The two series of topics are arranged according to a similar plan, so that each year a similar scheme of activities may be followed, though the details of subject-matter are different. It is important that this difference in subject-matter should be clearly recognised, so that the second year of the course may not be a mere repetition of the first. There should not be any attempt to carry out the whole programme of work in one year; there is ample material for two years' teaching, provided that the children are given scope for active participation and expression.

Juniors

Where the class is very small the teacher may feel that the best plan is to take the whole of the junior syllabus as a four-year course. It is possible to do this if the story element is emphasised, and if the material in the third and fourth years is treated in a simple way. The advantages of this method are obvious: the teacher's work is simplified, and the family spirit of the small group is maintained. As in a family, each child takes what it can from the narratives: but the activities must be varied according to age and ability. One of the dangers incident to the method is the possible boredom of the older children; this is perhaps more likely to occur in the larger class where there is a greater consciousness of age groups. To meet the needs of such classes, where it is felt desirable to give the older children a sense of responsibility, the following suggestions are made:

A. *New Testament*

    (1) For the children from 7 to 10 a three-year course based on the life of Jesus, following that designed for children aged 7 to 9 and sections I and IV of the course for children aged 9 to 11.

    (2) For the children of 10, who are capable of individual study, sections III and V of the course designed for children aged 9 to 11 will provide material of a type which can be arranged for them to study on their own; the individual work might be undertaken on one or more days in each week, other days being devoted to work with the class as a whole.

B. *Old Testament*

A four-year scheme of stories from the Old Testament, based on the syllabus. There should be no attempt at chronology, and the story element should predominate. Sometimes it may not come amiss for the teacher to retell some of the children's favourite stories; but the general aim should be to introduce as many as possible of the stories suggested in the syllabus for the four years, particularly the stories that are less commonly known.

THE SINGLE TEACHER SCHOOL

The teacher who is responsible for all the children from 5 to 11 has a particularly difficult task in the Scripture lesson. The practice of teaching all the children together cannot be recommended as a general rule, though there will be many occasions when, for purposes of worship and festival celebrations, the unity of the school will be emphasised by all the children being treated as members of a large family. It is obvious, however, that with regard to the content of lessons the older children are capable of understanding much that is only confusing to the little child, and the younger children need, both in the manner of presentation and in the actual language used by the teacher, a simplicity which the older child may resent.

The teacher is recommended, therefore, to keep to the normal division of the school into an infant group and a junior group, and as far as possible to follow in each group the suggestions made for teachers in small schools. This involves considerable preparation on the part of the teacher, and it is recognised that under these conditions far less ground can be covered than is suggested by the syllabus, since the working pace is of necessity much slower than in the large school. The teacher is therefore advised to select parts from each section of the course rather than to attempt the whole.

In each group the method will be chiefly that of story-telling by the teacher, and individual and group activities by the children. Both infants and juniors must be trained to employ themselves without supervision, since the teacher must be able as a story-teller to devote periods of at least fifteen minutes' undivided attention to one group. The planning of activities is thus one of the most important parts of the teacher's work, and it should be done on a generous scale: for instance, the teacher who thinks it desirable for infants to make pictures will find that the children are far more absorbed in the painting of a large picture than in the pencil drawing of a small one; or, children who are generously supplied with clay or plasticine to make a comprehensive model of an Eastern home, or a sheep-fold with many sheep, have a more satisfying activity than those who can make only one small water-pot, or lamp, or sheep. Frequent acting of stories by the two groups is particularly recommended; one group may sometimes present its drama to the other; and it is often necessary in very small schools for the groups to amalgamate for acting. This is another way in which the sense of the family is kept alive.

Finally, the teacher should feel a considerable amount of freedom to experiment and to plan the work on whatever lines she has found most successful in a small school, provided that the needs of the children of different ages are not overlooked and that the underlying purpose of the infant and the junior sections of the syllabus is achieved.

THE LANGUAGE OF THE BIBLE

Of the Bible as literature the late Sir Arthur Quiller-Couch, who was a member of the Committee which drew up the first *Cambridgeshire Syllabus of Religious Teaching* in 1924, has written:

> I shall ask you first to assent with me, that the authorised version of the Holy Bible is, as a literary achievement, one of the greatest in our language; nay, with the possible exception of the complete works of Shakespeare, the very greatest. You will certainly not deny this. As little, or less, will you deny that more deeply than any other book— more deeply even than all the writings of Shakespeare—far more deeply—it has influenced our literature:
>
> Thine eyes shall behold the King in his beauty: they shall behold the land that is very far off.
> And a man shall be as a hiding place from the wind, and a covert from the tempest; as rivers of water in a dry place, as the shadow of a great rock in a weary land....
> So when this corruptible shall have put on incorruption, and this mortal shall have put on immortality....
>
> When a nation has achieved this manner of diction, these rhythms for its dearest beliefs, a literature is surely established. Wyclif, Tyndale, Coverdale and others before the forty-seven, had wrought. The Authorised Version, setting a seal on all, set a seal on our national style. It has cadences homely and sublime, yet so harmonises them that the voice is always one. Simple men—holy and humble men of heart like Izaak Walton and Bunyan—have their lips touched and speak to the homelier tune. Proud men, scholars—Milton, Sir Thomas Browne— practise the rolling Latin sentences; but upon the rhythms of our Bible they too fall back—'The great mutations of the world are acted, or time may be too short for our designs.' 'Acquaint thyself with the Choragium of the Stars.' 'There is nothing immortal but immortality.' The precise man Addison cannot excel one parable in brevity or in heavenly clarity; the two parts of Johnson's antithesis come to no more than this: 'Our Lord has gone up to the sound of a trump; with the sound of a trump our Lord has gone up.' The Bible controls its enemy Gibbon as surely as it haunts the curious music of a light sentence of Thackeray. It is in everything we see, hear, feel, because it is in us, in our blood....
>
> These cadences, these phrases have for three hundred years exercised a most powerful effect, by association of ideas, by the accreted memories

of our race enwrapping connotation around a word, a name—say the name of *Jerusalem*, or the name *Sion*:

> And they that wasted us required of us mirth, saying,—
> Sing us one of the songs of Sion.
> How shall we sing the Lord's song in a strange land?
> If I forget thee, O Jerusalem, let my right hand forget her cunning!

It must be known to you that these words can affect men to tears who never connect them in thought with the actual geographical Jerusalem, who connect it in thought merely with a quite different native home from which they are exiles. Here and there some one man may feel a similar emotion over Landor's

> Tanagra, think not I forget....

But the word Jerusalem will strike twenty men twentyfold more poignantly; for to each it names the city familiar in spirit to his parents when they knelt, and to their fathers before them; not only the city which was his nursery and yet lay just beyond the landscape seen from its window; its connotation includes not only what the word Rome has meant, and ever must mean, to thousands on thousands setting eyes for the first time on *The City*: but it holds too some hint of the New Jerusalem, the city of twelve gates before the vision of which St John fell prone:

> Ah, my sweet home, Hierusalem,
> Would God I were in thee!
> Thy Gardens and thy gallant walks
> Continually are green:
> There grows such sweet and pleasant flowers
> As nowhere else are seen.
> Quite through the streets with pleasant sound
> The flood of life doth flow;
> Upon whose banks on every side
> The wood of Life doth grow....

You cannot get away from these connotations, accreted through your own memories and your fathers': as neither can you be sure of getting free of any great literature in any tongue, once it has been written....

If that be true, or less than gravely overstated; if the English Bible hold this unique place in our literature; if it be at once a monument, an example and (best of all) a well of English undefiled, no stagnant water, but quick, running, curative, refreshing, vivifying; may we not agree to require the weightiest reason why our instructors should continue to hedge in the temple and pipe the fountain off in professional conduits, forbidding it to irrigate freely our ground of study?[1]

[1] Sir Arthur Quiller-Couch, *On the Art of Reading*.

Our syllabus is intended to open the temple, by no means to hedge it up. Perhaps the difficulty of selecting the best words and matter from so large a book has had something to do with former shyness. The syllabus is intended as a guide to selection.

MAKING THE BIBLE FAMILIAR TO CHILDREN

Infants

The young child's delight in rhythmical language has for a long time been recognised as an important factor in his education. He learns nursery rhymes, simple poems and songs without effort. In his religious education the hymns of the morning service have a similar appeal; singing them with the teacher, he soon learns the hymns most frequently sung. If laboured teaching is found necessary, it probably indicates that the hymn is unsuitable and too difficult. For these hymns must be chosen with great care; many so-called children's hymns are sentimental, others meaningless to small children; while the thought should be simple and the language direct, some hymns strain after this simplicity and achieve mere childishness. Children's hymns should be short; if a longer hymn is used, it is wise to select a few verses only for the children to sing. Here are a few good children's hymns on different themes:

> 'Jesus, tender Shepherd, hear me....'
> 'Away in a manger....'
> 'Father, we thank Thee for the night....'
> 'God make my life a little light....'
> 'I love God's tiny creatures....'

Most children will learn hymns readily because they want to learn them. Many odd phrases and verses of Scripture will be as readily learnt because they fall easily from the tongue and strike pleasantly on the ear. But it is a pity that the matter should end there. If some motive can be found for speaking certain passages, it will give purpose and direction to the children's activity, bringing them nearer to the spirit and meaning of the words they learn. Often there is a dramatic motive which can easily be utilised, as in the story of the child Samuel or the parable of the Lost Sheep, where the search in many places—largely a matter of dumb show—finds a natural conclusion in the words 'Rejoice with me for I have found my sheep which was lost'.

Apart from such simple dramatic passages there is not a great deal in the Bible that is suitable for memorising by the young child. In addition it should also be remembered how children may be misled by strange words, or by familiar words used in a strange way, as in 'Suffer little children, and forbid them not, to come unto me', which children often learn, but whose meaning they misapprehend on account of the prominence of the word 'suffer': there is a similar danger in the twenty-third Psalm, 'Though I walk through the valley of the shadow of death...', 'Thou preparest a table before me...', 'Thou anointest my head with oil...my cup runneth over...'. Probably there is no complete poem in the Bible suitable for such young children, and it is better for them to memorise shorter passages. If such sentences as 'I am the good Shepherd: the good Shepherd giveth his life for the sheep' form part of the language of the teacher, they will also become part of the child's storehouse of remembered sentences.

Junior and Secondary

The dramatic work and the simple memory work of the infant class will be extended during the early years of the junior school: but as the children become older they need more scope for their growing powers of memory and of speech. Some children have a great facility for memorising, but there is a danger of its becoming a barren occupation if the passage memorised has not been properly understood or appreciated. One very effective method of arousing the enthusiasm of older children for the language of the Bible is that of choral speaking. If there is discussion and experiment by class and teacher as to whether a passage is most suited to antiphonal, unison or group speaking, there will often develop a feeling for a passage that comes near to real understanding. The speakers gain much help if the speaker is a good conductor.

Sometimes certain outstanding qualities in a passage are made clearer if it is presented in a fresh way. If the story of the house on the rock and the house on the sand are written out in two columns, with corresponding lines opposite, the parallelism of the story is emphasised. In attempting to speak the passage in one group or in two contrasted groups, children not only find enjoyment in the Biblical language but become aware of the truth it enshrines. After speaking it a few times with the copy in front of them children will find they can discard it and concentrate on the speaking.

The parallel stories of the Lost Sheep and the Lost Coin could similarly be spoken in two groups. These stories illustrate the difference between the treatment that is suitable for infants and that suitable for older juniors and for seniors. Infants will come to know and understand the stories best through miming them and giving in speech only the shout of joy on the discovery of the lost treasure. Older children, who have outgrown their delight in spontaneous acting and have not yet learnt the art of symbolic miming, will gain more satisfaction from speaking the two passages.

Many of the Psalms give excellent opportunities for choral speaking, although different forms of treatment will be suitable for different Psalms. The first verse of Psalm civ, for example, lends itself to a full chorus; subsequent verses to antiphonal treatment of their two halves by two groups; the whole Psalm is probably too long for children to speak except in two sections, but a concluding chorus may be found for the last three verses of the Psalm. Psalm cxxxvi could be interpreted by an individual speaker who proclaims the great acts of God—'To him that made great lights...' with the full chorus giving the regularly repeated refrain 'for his mercy endureth for ever'. All the pilgrim songs lend themselves to chorus work. Psalms xlii and xliii form one complete song, with a four-line refrain ('Why art thou cast down, O my soul?...') coming at the end of every stanza. In Psalm xxiv, the ceremonial procession, with the presence of Jehovah signified by the Ark that was to be carried into the Temple, is described in dramatic language that appeals even to younger children: the series of questions and answers makes a kind of liturgical dialogue. Sometimes the whole body of people seems to speak together; then there is division, and the dramatic dialogue is given by two groups. A child cannot take part in a dramatic rendering of a Psalm such as this without being the richer for it.

Teachers will find that many passages even of pure narrative can be treated in a similar way, and there will always be interest in discovering what is the best method for a particular story.

If such speaking of the Scriptures is undertaken it is not necessary to set passages for children to memorise. The passages which they learn to speak well together will become part of their experience. There will be occasions when they need to speak them from memory, perhaps as part of the morning service, perhaps as part of a simple programme presented to another class. But even if they fail to become word perfect, they are becoming better acquainted with the Bible than they would be by the mere act of committing to memory a number of set passages.

Children can also practise individual reading from the Bible. St Matthew xiii has a collection of parables of varying lengths: individual children might practise reading their own set parable; there are some very short parables which might be given to the weaker readers.

The literature of the Bible is so comprehensive that there is scope for infinite variety in its treatment. Perhaps the finest service the teacher can render to the child in school is to help him to know and love the Bible. The methods suggested here may help to bring this about.

HISTORY, LEGEND AND MYTH

A historical narrative sets out to report events as they happened, though the reporter may unwittingly make mistakes.

A legend starts from events that happened, but contains elements which are not factually true; these legendary elements, however, may throw light upon the meaning attached to the events by those transmitting an account of them.

A myth is a folk-tale which did not begin with events at all, but expresses men's ideas and beliefs in story form.

All these types of narrative are found in the Bible, and it is important to distinguish between them, though the distinction may be a delicate one in any particular instance. In general, most parts of the Bible may be taken as genuinely historical sources, though they vary in their value as such. But there is also an element of legend and myth which should be recognised.

The story contained in a myth usually serves to account for the mysteries of nature or of human life, or to explain some rite or practice whose beginnings are unknown. Thus the ancient Greek myth in which Persephone, the daughter of Demeter, Mother Earth, was carried off to the underworld leaving her mother mourning, but was later restored to her in joyful reunion, tells how vegetation languishes at the onset of winter, but in spring rises again to new life. At the same time the myth served as an 'explanation' of the rites performed at the Eleusinian mysteries, the most famous and solemn of all the religious festivals of ancient Greece, but whose origin was lost in antiquity. When the ritual developed a more spiritual aspect it appears (though the details are not certain) that those initiated into the mysteries went through ceremonies of purification and of communion with the divinity, in which an assurance of immortality was given. The Persephone myth was then reinterpreted as symbolising human resurrection; man dies like the grass, but rises again. A similar myth underlies the folk-tale of John Barleycorn, commemorated by Burns; but later explanations have caused us to forget most of our English myths, or tame them into fairy stories. But there never was a historical John Barleycorn, nor was there a woman called Demeter who sought for her child Persephone. A myth has no date; it belongs to 'once upon a time'.

A legend has a quite different origin. It begins with the memory of something that actually happened or of a person who actually lived, whose character the legend serves to illustrate. Many legends refer to such ancient times that it is only possible to guess what originally happened. But any event that strikes the imagination, like the turn of the tide of war at Mons in The First World War or the absence of a German cross-Channel invasion in 1940, or any person of vivid character, like King Alfred, Dr Johnson or Queen Victoria, may give rise to legends. Such legends may throw valuable light on history, since they reveal the common impression made by persons and events. In dim and remote ages legends may have some historical value, if treated critically. Thus the legends of the Trojan War, and of King Arthur, which were at one time dismissed as either fictions or myths, are now generally recognised to refer, in however disguised a form, to actual historical events.

In the Bible the element of myth proper is small in comparison with other religious literatures. The stories of Adam and Eve, of the sons of God and the daughters of men, of the Flood, and of the Tower of Babel, are comparable to the mythologies of other peoples. The description of the Flood, inasmuch as it doubtless contains reminiscences of a local inundation in Mesopotamia attested by archaeological evidence, might be described as legendary, but the idea of a universal flood, and the regeneration of the human race through the survivors, is found in the mythologies of many peoples, and has nothing historical about it. The story of the tower of Babel may have been suggested by some ancient Ziggurat, or 'sky-scraper' temple in Babylonia, but the story of men who defied heaven and were confounded is another widespread theme of myths, such as the ancient Greek tale of the Titans piling mountain on mountain to storm the home of the gods. It is not a story of something that happened, but an account of the sort of thing which always happens when man's overweening pride and self-confidence lead him to forget his dependence upon God.

Beyond this short list pure myth is hardly to be found in the Old Testament, though there are many echoes of a forgotten mythology, especially in the poetical books. When the creation story in the first chapter of Genesis is compared with the Babylonian creation myth it can be seen that both had a similar origin, but the comparison also shows how the purely mythical element has been refined away in the Biblical account. It may be described as a philosophical poem, declaring that all things have their origin in God and that the works of his hands are good. Even the other myths, though they retain their mythical form, have been given a deeper meaning by the prophetic thinkers whose work lies behind the Old Testament narratives. The story of the Fall explains the existence of evil as the result of disobedience to God, and the story of the Flood leads up to the idea, represented in God's covenant with Noah, that the whole life of man and beast is established according to divine law and providence.

The element of legend is much larger in the Old Testament; the dividing line between the legendary and the historical is frequently imperceptible. The stories of the patriarchs must be described as legendary, although they preserve a 'folk-memory' of events in the remote past. They undoubtedly refer to actual migrations and adventures of the primitive Hebrew clans during the second millennium B.C. The cutting loose from Mesopotamia, the wanderings in Canaan and down to the frontiers of Egypt, the relations, partly friendly, partly hostile, with the settled inhabitants, the intermarriages with the original stock in Aram, the famines, the slave trade with Egypt, the digging of wells, the worshipping under sacred trees, the raising of sacred stones and pillars—all these have a basis in history. But the attachment of these stories to individuals, their picturesque and vivid detail, belong to the legendary development. But just as prophetic thinkers took the primitive myths and made them vehicles for religious lessons, so they similarly used the folk-tales of their people. Thus, in the story of Abraham, Lot and Sodom, there may be a memory of a Hebrew clan in the Cities of the Plain and of a disaster which overtook them. But the importance of the story lies in the portrait of a God of justice and mercy, and of human communication with Him, contained in the words put into the mouth of Abraham: 'Behold, I have taken upon myself to speak unto the Lord, which am but dust and ashes....Shall not the Judge of all the earth do right?' Legend, then, while it must not be confused with history, nevertheless has a value in revealing the impression made by persons and events, and in the use made of it at a later date by men of religious insight to convey certain truths.

With the Exodus we begin to find firmer historical footings; for the main events of this period are undoubtedly historical, though the form in which they are related is often legendary. The impressive figure of Moses has gathered about it a cycle of legends which emphasise his importance as a religious leader. It may even be said that it would have been difficult to bring home the outstanding significance of the religious developments associated with the name of Moses without this setting of legend—the burning bush, the parting of the sea, the pillar of fire and cloud, the supernatural events at Sinai and so forth. Each of these may have some historical nucleus of fact; but the real truth of Sinai is not (as some have suggested) a particularly severe thunderstorm or a volcanic eruption, but an affirmation of belief in One God and an assertion that He is concerned with right conduct: 'God spake these words and said, I am the Lord thy God....'

It is unnecessary to attempt to trace the division between legend and history in the later books. It is a fair general statement that for the period before the Exodus the facts of history must be recovered from an almost wholly legendary presentation; from the Exodus to the time of David much of the history is still embodied in legend, but there is an admixture of direct historical tradition, and even of first-hand record, such as in the Song of Deborah; from the time of David onwards we have a series of good, sometimes first-rate, historical documents, with occasional legendary embroidery, as in the stories of Elijah and Elisha.

In addition to myth and legend there are deliberately fictitious narratives such as the parables which occur frequently in the Gospels and occasionally in the Old Testament (Jotham, Nathan). No one would think of taking these for historical records. But it is probable that there are other fictitious narratives, notably that of Jonah. Jonah himself is a historical character (II Kings xiv. 25), but his adventures are a parable of the mission of Israel to the nations. The whole purpose of the story is to show how inevitable is God's call to Israel to evangelise the nations. In the same way the book of Ruth, in its present form, probably represents a later writing up of an older story as a counter to the exclusiveness of Ezra's marriage laws. But apart from parables expressly offered as such, deliberate fiction plays only a small part in the Bible.

It should now be clear that, so far as the main movement of the history is concerned, the Bible gives trustworthy information. Any idea that criticism shows it to be fundamentally untrustworthy is quite false. Critical scholarship has enabled us to place an even higher value on the Bible than before, since it has shown us how to evaluate its different parts more correctly.

The distinction between history, legend and myth should be in the mind of the teacher and affect the manner in which he deals with the stories. It should also be remembered that the question 'Is it true?' has more than one meaning. There is the truth of historical fact which is expected in a purely historical narrative. But there is also spiritual and moral truth, the truth of the kind which can be found, for example, in the creation story in the very first chapter of the Bible, when once we have ceased to ask from it a truth of historical fact to which it does not pretend.

'All the sweetness of religion is conveyed to the world by the hands of story-tellers and image-makers. Without their fictions the truths of religion would for the multitude be neither intelligible nor even apprehensible and the prophets would prophesy and the teachers teach in vain. And nothing stands between the people and the fictions except the silly falsehood that the fictions are literal truths, and that there is nothing in religion but fiction.' (BERNARD SHAW.)

MIRACLES IN THE NEW TESTAMENT

Our records show that among the early Christians the miraculous was considered as something which they had come to expect as part of the new way of life to which they had been introduced. 'I will not dare', wrote Paul, 'to speak of any things save those which Christ wrought through me, for the obedience of the Gentiles, by word and deed, in the power of signs and wonders, in the power of the Holy Spirit' (Romans xv. 18–19). Some twenty years later a Christian writer recalled how after salvation was first proclaimed by Jesus Christ, it 'was confirmed unto us by them that heard; God also bearing witness with them both by signs and wonders and by manifold powers, and by gifts of the Holy Spirit, according to his own will' (Hebrews ii. 3–4). We could not ask for better first-hand evidence that the early preaching of the Gospel was accompanied by events which were regarded as miraculous.

The place assigned to this aspect of the life of the Early Church is evident from these two passages, as well as from others. They are part of the work of the Holy Spirit. (Not the most important; they occupy a modest place in the middle of Paul's list of spiritual gifts in I Corinthians xii. 7–11.) The work of the Holy Spirit was taken as a sign and pledge that Christians were living a new life of direct contact with the power of God. That power showed itself in the increase of wisdom, knowledge, faith and, above all, love (I Corinthians xii. 31–xiii. 3). It seemed natural to early believers that where such power was abroad it should manifest itself also in remarkable works of healing and other 'miraculous' happenings, such as are related in Acts. With our present outlook upon the world, we are sometimes inclined to suspect that in such cases what actually happened might be susceptible, if we knew all the facts, of a 'natural' explanation. But even if we could reduce these 'miracles' to normal occurrences, we should still not have explained what made them for the early Christians tokens of the work of the Holy Spirit, namely, the powerful impression on those present that the power of God was there. In a religious sense a 'miracle' is not so much an inexplicable occurrence as one which brings an overwhelming sense of the very presence of God. Of course, if one does not believe that God really works upon men (if, that is to say, such expressions as 'answers to prayer', 'communion with God', 'divine guidance' are at best mere figures of speech), then one will say that this sense of the divine presence was a mistake, due to mass suggestion or what not. But if one believes in God then it is an impressive fact that such a man as Paul (who was no fool) did things and saw things done which convinced him that power came from God.

Miracles, then, in the New Testament, are associated with a new way of life, described as 'life in the Holy Spirit'. This new life was introduced by the coming of Jesus Christ. We should therefore expect that stories of miracles would have a place in the traditions about Him. Long before our Gospels were written the first Christian preachers were declaring that Jesus of Nazareth 'went about doing good, and healing all that were oppressed of the devil; for God was with him' (Acts x. 38). Critical analysis of the Gospels shows that the most primitive and authoritative parts of the tradition lying behind them contained miracle-stories. This or that particular story may, with good reason, be questioned; all of them were handed on by word of mouth for a long time, and everyone knows how easily a story is altered in the telling, especially if it is a wonderful story. But one thing is certain, that from the very beginning the story of Jesus was told as the story of one who performed miracles, and it was so told by those who, as we have seen, had experience of 'miraculous' occurrences in their own lives, and regarded them as tokens of a new way of life inaugurated by Jesus.

All the miracle-stories of the Gospels, whatever their individual value as records of actual events, bear witness to the convictions of the first Christians that the appearance of Jesus opened fresh channels of divine life to men. That is the true 'supernatural'. There can be no doubt that Jesus really was such a Person that His deeds convinced men of the presence and power of God, and this, in a religious sense, is what 'miracle' means.

Beyond this general significance of the miracle-stories as marking the beginning of a new way of life and as showing the powerful impression Jesus made upon His contemporaries, we can often consider these stories in the light in which they are presented in the Fourth Gospel; as 'signs', or symbols of a truth beyond the action itself. Thus John gives the story of the feeding of the multitude as a symbol of the 'Bread from Heaven'—the spiritual food given to those who come to Christ. It may well be that such a symbolical intention was sometimes in the mind of Jesus Himself. The prophets were accustomed to perform symbolical actions to enforce their words. Jeremiah, for instance, went about with a yoke on his neck, to signify that his people, with other nations, would fall under the yoke of Babylon (Jeremiah xxvii–xxviii). Jesus was regarded as 'one of the prophets'. His methods were like theirs. If now we recall that He told a parable of a great feast, to which guests were invited with the words 'Come, for all things are ready', it is no wild hypothesis that when He 'made the men sit down' and gave them food by the hands of His disciples (wherever the food come from), He was acting out His own parable, signifying by word and act alike that the new life of the Kingdom of God was now available for men. It is probable that we are very near to the original historical situation if we understand some at least of the miracle-stories as 'signs' in the prophetic sense.

If we go on to ask what exactly happened in each case we must recognise not only that our gospels are the outcome of a long process of oral tradition, but also that the stories in them were not told in the first place to gratify curiosity about what happened, but to illustrate and enforce the truth of the Gospel. Consequently, they do not give us the data which a modern historian would ask for. It is this that makes it precarious to attempt to reconstruct our own version of what happened. In order to make the stories more intelligible to our own minds, we are justified in using our imagination and in applying scientific knowledge where it appears to throw light on the gospels; some of the stories of healing and 'casting out demons', for example, can be better understood when illuminated by the findings of modern psychotherapy. But we must always remember that this is largely guesswork. Crude rationalisation, such as is often found in works of the last century, and sometimes even to-day, does not really help, and may obscure the primary intention of the story.

The chief difficulty encountered in treating the miracle-stories as records of fact lies in the widespread belief that 'miracles do not happen'. There is here a large philosophical problem. It is the problem of the nature of the universe. To attempt to deal with it in a few lines would be ludicrously misleading. Those who are seriously interested are recommended to study carefully books in which the whole philosophical bearings of the matter are explored.[1]

It is safe to say that serious thinkers are less inclined to-day than a generation ago to regard the question of miracles as closed. It is well to bear in mind what the conception of miracle in the New Testament really is. Miracles are not thought of as casual or arbitrary interferences with the order of nature, but merely as being among the indications of the appearance, in Jesus, of a new kind of relationship with God, in which His power was visibly at work among men. Christians believe that the coming of Jesus Christ was a unique event in the history of the world. Apart from any particular 'signs and wonders' it was a miracle in itself, since it brought God nearer to men than ever before.

So much is fundamental. But it is also a part of the body of Christian traditions that the exceptional character of the event was

---

[1] Such as *The Natural and the Supernatural*, by John Oman (C.U.P. 1931, 18s.); *The World and God*, by H. H. Farmer (Nisbet, 1935, 10s. 6d.); *Providence and the World Order*, by C. F. D'Arcy (Hodder and Stoughton, 1932, 6s.); *The Purpose of God*, by W. R. Matthews (Nisbet, 1935, 7s. 6d.); *Miracles*, by C. S. Lewis (Bles, 1947, 10s. 6d.).

revealed throughout in occurrences of an exceptional character on the physical plane. The evidence for these occurrences will not convince those who attribute no special significance to the life and death of Jesus. For those who do, the question is not whether the laws of nature can or cannot be suspended, but whether there is such an intimate connection between the spiritual and the physical that the one affects the other. That is a philosophical question. Our individual faith as Christians does not depend upon its solution; those who answer the question in the negative may still be Christians. Those who answer it in the affirmative believe that the spiritual and physical orders interact within one universe under the governance of God and His laws, and that the Gospel narratives, properly interpreted, contribute to the understanding of the true nature of that universe.

THE ARTIST AND THE CHRISTIAN FAITH

No one has made a bigger contribution to the Christian faith than the Artist. When we think of the prose, the poetry and the music, the architecture, the sculpture and the painting, which have illuminated the Christian faith in Europe, we realise something of the grandeur of this endowment. We only have to mention Dante, Milton, George Herbert, Blake, the Authorised Version and the Book of Common Prayer, John Bunyan, Palestrina, Bach, Handel, Mantagna, Fra Angelico, Botticelli, Leonardo da Vinci, Raphael, Michelangelo, the cathedrals at Chartres, Durham, Lincoln and Ely, and King's College Chapel, Cambridge —and we can but marvel at the wealth of this contribution to the Christian tradition made by artists in all forms of expression. Such beauty is part of the Christian revelation, and as such, the teacher will attempt to convey something of it. These creations of the Christian artist must not, of course, be too much the subject of didactic treatment. But the appreciation, or indeed the love, of them by the teacher can be a very potent influence in teaching. At the same time we have to be careful not to press these grandeurs on children who are quite unprepared for them. Later on, as boys and girls grow up, there may be chances of their developing such appreciation naturally and spontaneously by coming into contact with, or catching an enthusiasm from, teacher or friend.

With older boys and girls, and perhaps with younger children too, the work of the painter is likely to be the most accessible avenue to the glories of Christian art. Such pictures will normally have to be seen in the form of reproductions. Many pictures have been printed as reproductions either singly or as illustrations to books on the work of various artists, and though reproductions must never be confused with the originals they do serve as pointers. If such reproductions and books can be obtained, boys and girls will have the chance of seeing some of the noblest renderings of the Nativity and of the Mother and Child. Thus the object should be to enable as many children as possible before they leave school to come into contact with the great tradition of Christian art by knowing some of the pictures of great European painters.

Unfortunately very few contemporary artists use directly religious subjects. The inexpensive books of pictures published for use in connection with Scripture teaching are not in any sense works of art. They are without true dignity, crude in colour and sentimental in conception. Let us therefore stick to the reproductions of the Masters, and if we want to give instruction on the Palestinian landscape, use photographs, films and film-strips.

Any pictures illustrating the Bible should be true to what we know of the person or incident concerned. The convention that the majority of men of Bible times must appear to be between sixty and seventy years old is one to be condemned. The disciples were young men and Jesus himself was young and vigorous. The background of the picture may be Palestinian or Italian or Flemish, but the figure of Christ should suggest someone who could live a strenuous life of prayer and action.

It should also be made clear, in showing a picture of a Biblical subject, that it is someone's interpretation of the event and not an authentic record of it; it is the artist's impression, the mental picture he has seen and strives to make concrete. A picture may be accurate in historical detail but false in its whole conception, or on the other hand it may contain inaccuracies but convey a spiritual and artistic sincerity which far outweighs the departure from literal accuracy. If this is pointed out to children they can appreciate it.

There are some incidents in the Bible which only a great artist can picture adequately, for example, the Temptation or the Transfiguration. If, as we believe, the Temptation was a spiritual experience, when our Lord reviewed the work before Him and rejected the temptation to win people by quick and easy means, then an illustration is apt to be unsatisfactory and it may be better to give the lesson without it. Most representations of the Ascension are unsatisfactory. The Bible narrative does not say 'Jesus went up and up and up' (as one teacher described it), but that 'a cloud received Him out of their sight'. We do not know the nature of the cloud, which is not to be regarded as a physical cloud, but rather as the Shekinah, the glory of the Lord, which received Him. Here again it may be better to use no pictures.

Care needs to be taken in showing pictures which may alarm children. No one who understands the impressionable nature of a child's mind would willingly allow him to see horrifying or distressing sights. Pictures of the Crucifixion, if shown at all, need to be shown with extreme care. Many teachers feel that a reproduction of any picture of the Crucifixion should never be shown to children under ten years of age, but as children are likely to see either a picture or a crucifix, other teachers think that it is better to deal with the matter at an early age.

Symbolism needs careful treatment with young children. They do not know, unless it is explained to them, that our Lord did not dress in white to distinguish Him from other people, or that He did not go about with a halo round his head. Except for the marks of His unique personality, to which many people were blind, He looked like any other Jew of His time, but artists have used various devices to emphasise His divinity. The halo is the most familiar, so familiar indeed that we are apt to forget how strange it is to children.

Biblical subjects have a particular visual appeal for children, and the paints and large paper which are often regarded as materials exclusively for 'Art' can well be used for expressing their own visual ideas of these subjects. Indeed these simple and naïve paintings by children often share, in their small way, the dignity and sincerity of the old masters more truly than the 'pretty-pretty' Scripture pictures which are to-day thought to be suitable for showing to children.

The following suggestions give some indication of the kinds of activity which are desirable:

(1) The making of books in which the children write and illustrate stories from the Bible. These may vary in elaboration according to age, and they may be small books made by individuals or large ones made by groups.

(2) Individual paintings.

(3) Co-operative paintings, e.g. on frieze paper, illustrating the story of Joseph, the Nativity, the Parables, or the Benedicite.

(4) Co-operative models, e.g. the making and lighting of a Christmas crib, using clay, wood and other materials.

All of the above apply particularly to the Infant and Junior stage, in which activity is so important.

The products of children should never be *compared* with reproductions of the work of adult artists.

Reproductions and photographs need not always be large enough to display singly to the whole class; it is often preferable to hand round smaller ones, or use may be made of an epidiascope, films or film-strips where possible. Books of reproductions should always be available for older children.

Teachers are advised to obtain from the Institute of Christian Education the selected list of illustrations for use with Scripture teaching drawn up for the use of teachers.[1] The list, which is comprehensive and also gives information concerning films, film-strips and epidiascopes, should be used in the light of what has been said above. Teachers who feel uncertain about the choice of pictures should seek the advice of a professional artist or art teacher.

[1] *Selected List of Illustrations for use in connection with Scripture Teaching* (3rd edition 1947), published by the Institute of Christian Education, 46 Gordon Square, London, W.C. 1, price 1s. (6d. to members of the Institute). Parts of the above Note are based upon the introductory section of this publication.

Religion is the vision of something which stands beyond, behind, and within, the passing flux of immediate things; something which is real, and yet waiting to be realised; something which is a remote possibility, and yet the greatest of present facts; something that gives meaning to all that passes, and yet eludes apprehension; something whose possession is the final good, and yet is beyond all reach; something which is the ultimate ideal, and the hopeless quest.

The immediate reaction of human nature to the religious vision is worship. Religion has emerged into human experience mixed with the crudest fancies of barbaric imagination. Gradually, slowly, steadily the vision recurs in history under nobler form with clearer expression. It is the one element in human experience which persistently shows an upward trend. It fades and then recurs. But when it renews its force, it recurs with an added richness and purity of content. The fact of the religious vision, and its history of persistent expansion, is our one ground for optimism. Apart from it, human life is a flash of occasional enjoyments lighting up a mass of pain and misery, a bagatelle of transient experience.

A. N. WHITEHEAD
Science and the Modern World

SOME BOOKS FOR REFERENCE

The following list is limited to standard works, large or small, which are likely to be found in Teachers', Borough, or County Libraries, or will readily be added by Librarians on the request of teachers. The list is designed to meet the needs of teachers who wish for further information concerning a particular part of the Bible or a particular aspect of Christianity. For convenience of reference, each section of the list is arranged alphabetically according to author, but it offers a choice of simpler or more advanced books, those of the simpler kind being indicated by an asterisk. Another reason for including rather a large number of books in the list is that, with books in short supply, and even new editions rapidly becoming out of print, where one particular book is unobtainable, an alternative may be available. A book has not been omitted from the list, in most cases, simply because it is out of print; teachers may be able to obtain a copy from a library or a second-hand copy, and there is always the hope that publishers will reprint.

The need of fuller information and the problem of keeping this up to date is now met by the Institute of Christian Education,[1] The Institute enrols teachers as members for a small subscription and in return offers them help and advice concerning books, films, gramophone records, daily worship and the variety of questions pupils ask their teachers. Full information may be obtained from the Secretary. The Institute's Library Committee is composed of acting teachers and Biblical scholars. It issues a bibliography, classified and annotated and based upon the generally recognised age-grouping of pupils from nursery school to sixth form; upon the successive sections into which the literature of the Bible falls (e.g. Background, Prophets, Gospels, St Paul, etc.); and upon the variety of aspects of religious education with which the teacher is concerned (e.g. Psychology of Religion in Childhood and Adolescence, Worship, etc.). Reviews of recent books are a special feature of the Quarterly Journal, *Religion in Education* (S.C.M. Press, 2s. per copy, of all booksellers, or 4s. 9d. per annum, post free), free to members of the Institute.

[1] 46 Gordon Square, London, W.C. 1.

The following addresses may be found useful:

The Religious Drama League. The Memorial Hall, 26 Farringdon Road, London, E.C. 1.

The Religious Drama Society. S.P.C.K. House, Northumberland Avenue, London, W.C. 2.

The Christian Cinema and Religious Film Society. 6 Eaton Gate, Westminster, S.W. 1.

The British Film Institute. 164 Shaftesbury Avenue, London, W.C. 2.

Teachers may also find it useful to get in touch with their denominational Sunday School departments.

BIBLES

Authorised Version. Clear-type edition. Oxford University Press, 5s. 6d.

Authorised Version. Clear-type edition. Cambridge University Press, 5s. 6d.

Revised Version. Clear-type edition. Oxford University Press, 7s. 6d.

Revised Version. Clear-type edition. Cambridge University Press, 7s. 6d.

Authorised Version with Apocrypha. Cambridge University Press. 7s. 6d.

Authorised Version with Apocrypha. Oxford University Press, 7s. 6d.
In smaller type.

The Apocrypha. Oxford University Press, 4s.

The Apocrypha. Cambridge University Press, 5s.

Revised Version. British and Foreign Bible Society, 5s.
In large type and paragraph form; an excellent edition for schools.

Revised Version with Apocrypha. Oxford and Cambridge University Press, 16s.

With references and marginal readings. A Bible of this type is strongly recommended for the teacher's own use.

Revised Version. American Standard edition. Oxford and Cambridge University Press.

MODERN VERSIONS AND ARRANGEMENTS

DAVIES, J. B. THOMSON. *The Heart of the Bible.* Allen and Unwin, 1936. 3 vols. 5*s.* each.

Contains the text in the chronological order of the original documents, with interspersed paragraphs explaining the historical growth of the Old and New Testaments. The school library should contain a copy.

MOFFATT, J. *A New Translation of the Bible.* Hodder and Stoughton, 1926. 21*s.* upwards.

MOFFATT, J. *The New Testament* (4*s.* 6*d.*), *the Psalms* (3*s.*), *the Prophets* (3*s.* 6*d.*). Hodder and Stoughton, 1938.

WEYMOUTH, R. F. *The New Testament in Modern Speech.* Clarke, 1934. 4*s.* upwards.

WILSON, R. MERCER. *The Book of Books.* Lutterworth Press, 1938. 5*s.*

Based upon the Authorised Version but incorporating renderings from Tyndale, the Revised Version, and other great translations, while it is so printed in fine type with paragraphing and cross-headings as to make it very suitable for school use.

WRIGLEY, F. E. *The Old Testament in the light of Modern Scholarship.* Independent Press, 1944. 3*s.*

Similar in treatment to the foregoing.

Translations of Old Testament Books into Colloquial Speech. National Adult School Union. Average price 1*s.* each.

Admirable translations made by eminent scholars.

SHORT BIBLES

The following are widely used:

The Cambridge Senior Bible. Cambridge University Press, 1945. 3*s.* 6*d.*

The Children's Bible. Cambridge University Press, 1947. 2*s.* 9*d.*

The Little Children's Bible. Cambridge University Press, 1947. 1*s.* 6*d.*

The Cambridge Shorter Bible. Cambridge University Press, 1928. 4s. 6d.

The three foregoing arranged by A. NAIRNE, A. QUILLER COUCH and T. R. GLOVER.

The Little Bible. Oxford University Press, 1931. 3s. 9d.

A selection according with the Leicestershire and Kent Syllabuses, and containing Notes.

A Short Bible. Edited by V. J. K. BROOK, A. A. DAVID, W. H. FYFE and A. E. LYNAM. Blackwell, 1946. 4s. 3d.

ABOUT THE BIBLE

(a) HISTORY

★KENYON, SIR FREDERIC G. *The Story of the Bible.* Murray, 1936. 3s. 6d.

A simple account of the manuscripts, versions and translations.

KENYON, SIR FREDERIC G. *The Bible and Modern Scholarship.* Murray, 1948. 3s. 6d.

MOULTON, W. F., abridged by A. W. HARRISON. *The History of the English Bible.* Epworth Press, 1937. 2s. 6d.

More detailed in its narrative of the development from Wyclif's Version to the Revised Version.

ROBINSON, H. WHEELER (editor). *The Bible in its Ancient and English Versions.* Oxford University Press, 1940. 15s.

(b) CONTENTS

★BARCLAY, G. *The Making and Meaning of the Bible.* S.C.M. Press, 1937. 2s. 6d.

An excellent simple first study of the subject.

DODD, C. H. *The Authority of the Bible.* Nisbet, 1928. 12s. 6d.

Deals lucidly with the growth and contents of the Biblical books and with that quality in them summed up by the word inspiration.

DODD, C. H. *The Bible To-day.* Cambridge University Press, 1946. 7s. 6d.

Presents the Bible as a unity of diverse writings which constitute a revelation of God in history.

★ Indicates books of the simpler kind.

RICHARDSON, A. *A Preface to Bible Study.* S.C.M. Press, 1943. 3s. 6d.

Written to help the reader to find his way about the Bible and to understand the difference between the Bible and other religious books.

*SKINNER, CONRAD. *Concerning the Bible.* Low. Revised 1939. 7s. 6d. (School Edition in strong paper covers, 4s. 6d.)

See reference on p. 84. Deals with the construction, contents, canon and history of the Bible, and discusses revelation and inspiration.

COMMENTARIES, DICTIONARIES AND CONCORDANCES

EISELEN, F. C. *The Abingdon Commentary.* Epworth Press, 1929. 32s. 6d.

One of the most readable commentaries.

GORE, BISHOP CHARLES. *A New Commentary on Holy Scripture.* S.P.C.K., 1929. 25s.

By Anglican scholars; includes the Apocrypha.

*MARTIN, H. *The Teacher's Commentary.* S.C.M. Press, 1932. 12s. 6d.

With maps and illustrations; prepared by teachers for teachers, with articles on special subjects as well as commentary.

PEAKE, A. S. *Commentary on the Bible.* Nelson, 1948. 25s.

Closely packed with detail.

Clarendon Bible. Oxford University Press, 1936. Old Testament vols. 7s. 6d. each; New Testament vols. different prices.

All the Old Testament volumes are excellent; the first volume provides an outline of the history of the people, the literature and the religious ideas, while the remaining five group the literature under the periods from Abraham to the time of Christ. The books of the New Testament are dealt with in separate volumes.

Moffatt New Testament Commentary. 17 Volumes, various authors. Hodder and Stoughton, 1928. 10s. 6d. each

Though not all the volumes are equal in merit, most will be found valuable by the teacher; the text is that of Moffatt's translation.

The Handbook of Christian Teaching. S.P.C.K. Reprinting. 8s. 6d.

Intended to help teachers in the moral and spiritual interpretation of the Bible to the extent that is legitimate without being 'distinctive of any religious formulary' on the one hand, but which is basic to denominational instruction on the other.

* Indicates books of the simpler kind.

Helps to the Study of the Bible. Oxford University Press, 1931. 8s. 6d.

Contains a useful short concordance, as well as a good deal of classified reference material. The introduction to the Biblical books has been brought up to date in the 1931 edition.

HASTINGS, J. *Dictionary of the Bible.* (One volume.) T. and T. Clark, 1909. 32s.

Most useful for constant reference.

MAJOR, H. D. A., MANSON, T. W. and WRIGHT, C. J. *The Mission and Message of Jesus.* Nicholson and Watson. 25s.

'An Exposition of the Gospels in the Light of Modern Research.' An outstanding book of current scholarship, valuable for frequent reference.

MANSON, T. W. (editor). *A Companion to the Bible.* T. and T. Clark, 1939. 16s.

Without exaggeration indispensable to the teacher; a brilliant and lucid compendium, by distinguished scholars, of modern knowledge concerning the literature, history, archaeology and religious content of the Bible and Apocrypha.

A Short Concordance for Schools. Nelson.

CRUDEN, A. *Complete Concordance to the Old and New Testaments.* Lutterworth Press, 1942. 15s.

YOUNG, R. *Analytical Concordance of the Bible.* Lutterworth Press, 1943. 45s.

The best English Concordance for the scholar, in which the English references are arranged under the original Hebrew and Greek words.

MAPS AND ATLASES

Wall Atlas of Bible Lands. Philip (George).

Set of eight maps on cloth, on one roller 78s.; on cloth with eyelets and dissected to fold 85s.; on cloth roller varnished, 12s. 6d. each, dissected 11s. 6d. each. Especially useful are No. 3 'Syria, Mesopotamia and the Persian Empire'; No. 6 'Palestine in the time of Christ'; and No. 8 'Modern Palestine, Physical'.

A New Scripture Atlas. Philip (George). 1s. 6d. (paper).

Contains sixteen coloured plates with 41 maps and plans: size 11×9 in.; convenient for desk use.

New Scripture Atlas. S.P.C.K. 2s.

The Westminster Smaller Bible Atlas. S.C.M. Press, 1947. 2s. 6d.

Contains sixteen coloured maps; convenient for desk use.

* Indicates books of the simpler kind.

WRIGHT, G. E. and FILSON, F. V. *The Westminster Historical Atlas of the Bible.* S.C.M. Press, 1947. 25s.

The best atlas for reference. It contains 33 coloured maps, 77 illustrations and 78 pages of letter-press of archaeological, geographical and historical information from the earliest times to A.D. 337.

BIBLICAL BACKGROUND

*ENTWISTLE, MARY. *The Bible Guidebook.* S.C.M. Press, 1947. 8s. 6d.

Contains simple and detailed information concerning Biblical manners and customs, with suggestions for blackboard illustrations and for handwork.

GLOVER, T. R. *The Ancient World.* Penguin, 1945. 1s. 6d.

Gives a historical background from the early Greeks to the Christian Roman Empire.

NEIL, J. *Everyday Life in the Holy Land.* S.P.C.K., 1920. 15s.

Descriptive, with illustrations.

*SANDERS, E. M. *The Holy Land*—the Land, the People and their Work. Philip (George), 1937, 1938. Book I in two parts, 1s. 9d. and 2s. 1d.; Book II 2s. 9d.

Letterpress, photographs and maps for junior pupils.

SMITH, SIR GEORGE ADAM. *The Historical Geography of the Holy Land.* Hodder and Stoughton. 26th edition, 1935. 25s.

The classic work on the subject.

OLD TESTAMENT

(a) INTRODUCTIONS

*EVANS, E. and ROBINSON, T. H. *The Bible, what it is and what is in it.* S.P.C.K., 1938. 5s.

A simple but thoroughly scholarly account of Biblical Geography, History and Religions, the books of the Bible (including the Apocrypha) and the teaching of the Bible about God, Man, Sin and Salvation; unduly conservative in the New Testament section; written in basic English for African and Asiatic Christians; a good class book for older boys and girls: useful to teachers.

OESTERLEY, W. O. E. and ROBINSON, T. H. *An Introduction to the Books of the Old Testament.* S.P.C.K., 1935. 10s. 6d.

See reference on p. 124.

* Indicates books of the simpler kind.

ROBINSON, H. WHEELER. *The Old Testament, Its Making and Its Meaning*. University of London Press, 1948. 7s. 6d.

A useful, scholarly and short introduction, which gives clearly and succinctly the conclusions generally accepted by scholars regarding the dates, authors, circumstances and purpose of the Old Testament books.

ROBINSON, H. WHEELER. *Inspiration and Revelation in the Old Testament*. Clarendon Press, 1946. 15s.

A study of God and nature, God and man, God and history, the inspiration of the prophet, revelation through the priest, in Wisdom and the Psalmists.

ROWLEY, H. H. *The Re-discovery of the Old Testament*. James Clarke, 1946. 10s. 6d.

An exposition of the deeper meaning of the Old Testament on the basis of recent scholarship.

(b) HISTORY AND ARCHAEOLOGY

*BAYNES, N. H. *Israel Among the Nations*. S.C.M. Press, 1927. 5s.

A short book admirably described by its title, and with a valuable bibliography.

*CAIGER, S. L. *The Old Testament and Modern Discovery*. S.P.C.K., 1938. 2s. 6d.

A good outline of Old Testament Archaeology.

CAIGER, S. L. *Bible and Spade*. Oxford University Press, 1936. 7s. 6d.

A simple, comprehensive and reliable account of the outcome of archaeological work in Bible lands during the present century.

OESTERLEY, W. O. E. and ROBINSON, T. H. *A History of Israel*. Oxford University Press, 1932. 2 vols., 21s. each.

Admirably arranged in sections with a full summary prefixed to each; covers the whole ground from earliest times to the fall of Jerusalem in A.D. 70, and affords the teacher a comprehensive view of all the essential facts, political, literary and religious. A standard work for reference.

RICHARDSON, G. H. *Biblical Archaeology, Its Use and Abuse*. Clarke, 1940. 3s. 6d.

A scholarly warning against uncritical interpretation of archaeological discoveries.

ROBINSON, H. WHEELER. *The History of Israel: its facts and factors*. Duckworth, 1947. 6s.

A condensed but clear and interesting study.

* Indicates books of the simpler kind.

SCHOFIELD, J. N. *The Historical Background of the Bible.* Nelson, 1948. 12s. 6d.

A useful general account.

*WOOLLEY, L. *Digging up the Past.* Pelican, 1937. 1s. 6d.

Relates Biblical archaeology to Greek and Roman.

*WOOLLEY, L. *Ur of the Chaldees.* Pelican, 1938. 1s. 6d.

A first-hand account of excavations revealing conditions in the time of Abraham.

(c) RELIGION

MATTHEWS, C. H. S. *The Roots of Religion and the Old Testament.* S.C.M. Press, 1935. 2s. 6d.

Fifth-form talks on primitive Hebrew religion and its development into that of the Prophets.

MONTEFIORE, C. G. *A Short Devotional Introduction to the Hebrew Bible.* Macmillan.

Extremely valuable as an exposition, from the liberal Jewish standpoint, of the essence of the Law, the Prophets and the Psalms.

*ROBINSON, H. WHEELER. *Religious Ideas of the Old Testament.* Duckworth, 1947. 6s.

Thorough, but not unduly technical.

SCHOFIELD, J. N. *The Religious Background of the Bible.* Nelson, 1944. 17s. 6d.

A useful general account.

*STEDMAN, A. R. *The Growth of Hebrew Religion.* Bell, 1936. 3s. 6d.

Simple and straightforward.

(d) THE PROPHETS

*DAVIES, J. B. THOMSON. *Heralds of God.* S.C.M. Press, 1942. 5s.

A simple introduction to the Hebrew prophets from Moses to John the Baptist.

ELMSLIE, W. A. L. *How Came Our Faith?* Cambridge University Press, 1948. 21s.

A scholarly attempt to show that the social gospel of Christianity is contained in the writings of the Old Testament prophets.

ROBINSON, T. H. *Prophecy and the Prophets in Ancient Israel.* Duckworth, 1948. 6s.

The best presentation of modern scholarship for the lay reader.

* Indicates books of the simpler kind.

SKINNER, JOHN. *Prophecy and Religion*. Cambridge University Press, 1940. 10*s*.

A study of prophecy with special reference to Jeremiah.

SMITH, SIR GEORGE ADAM. *The Book of Isaiah*. Hodder and Stoughton, 1927. 2 vols., 10*s*. 6*d*. each.

Contains illuminating translations and a wealth of vivid comment, rich in background material, of great service in teaching.

SMITH, SIR GEORGE ADAM. *The Book of the Twelve Prophets*. Hodder and Stoughton, 1928. 2 vols., 10*s*. 6*d*. each.

Similar to the foregoing.

★SUTCLIFFE, T. H. *The Prophetic Road to God*. S.P.C.K., 1937 3*s*. 6*d*.

A very simple introduction, but of considerable usefulness in teaching.

(*e*) THE EXILE AND AFTER

★BATHO, D. *The Birth of Judaism*. S.P.C.K., 1945. 5*s*.

Deals with the two and a half centuries from Jeremiah to the close of the Old Testament.

BEVAN, EDWYN. *Jerusalem under the High Priests*. Arnold, 1904. 8*s*. 6*d*.

A classical account of the Maccabees and their successors.

★BROWNE, L. E. *From Babylon to Bethlehem*. Heffer, 1926. 3*s*. 6*d*.

Outlines the events between the return from the Exile and the time of Christ.

CHARLES, R. H. *Religious Development between the Old and the New Testaments*. Home University Library, 1914. 5*s*.

A concise and fairly simple account of the origin and contents of the books in the Old Testament Apocrypha.

DRIVER, S. R. *Daniel*, in the Cambridge Bible for Schools. 1900.

Has a valuable introduction on apocalyptic literature.

★LUMB, WINIFRED. *Later Judaism*, a Text-book of Jewish History from 200 B.C. to A.D. 70. S.P.C.K., 1937. 1*s*.

RANKIN, O. S. *Israel's Wisdom Literature*. T. and T. Clark, 1936. 11*s*. 6*d*.

A valuable introduction to the Wisdom Literature.

★ Indicates books of the simpler kind.

NEW TESTAMENT

(a) INTRODUCTIONS

CLOGG, F. B. *An Introduction to the New Testament.* University of London Press, 1948. 8s. 6d.

Gives clearly and succinctly the conclusions generally accepted by scholars regarding the dates, authors, circumstances and purpose of the books of the New Testament.

(b) HISTORY AND ARCHAEOLOGY

*CAIGER, S. L. *Archaeology and the New Testament.* Cassell. Reprinting. 7s. 6d.

A companion volume to *Bible and Spade* on the Old Testament.

DEISSMAN, G. A. *Light from the Ancient East.* Translated by R. A. STRACHAN. Hodder and Stoughton, 1927. £2. 2s.

The standard work on the subject, well illustrated.

(c) THE GOSPELS

BLUNT, A. W. F. *The Gospels and the Critic.* Oxford University Press, 1936. 3s. 6d.

An admirable sketch of the growth and outcome of scholarly research, concise and illuminating.

*DODD, C. H. *How to Read the Gospels.* Church Assembly, 1948. 1s.

*JONES, MAURICE. *The Four Gospels.* S.P.C.K. Reprinting. 4s. 6d.

An account of their literary history and special characteristics.

RAWLINSON, A. E. J. *St Mark's Gospel.* Methuen, 1936.

In the *Westminster Commentaries* series.

*RICHARDSON, ALAN. *The Gospels in the Making.* S.C.M. Press, 1938. 5s.

An interestingly written and discriminating account for non-technical readers of how the Gospels came into existence, both source-criticism and form-criticism being brought under review.

*SMITH, JOSEPH D. *Synoptic Tables.* Berean Press, Birmingham, 1932. 2s. and 3s.

An index to parallel passages from which teacher or pupil can work out a chart, or make, from cheap Testaments, a full synopsis.

* Indicates books of the simpler kind.

STRACHAN, R. H. *The Fourth Gospel.* S.C.M. Press, 1943. 12s. 6d.
Popular but scholarly; a good book for the ordinary reader.

STREETER, B. H. *The Four Gospels.* Macmillan, 1936. 21s.
An advanced discussion from the standpoint of literary and historical criticism.

TAYLOR, VINCENT. *The Gospels: A Short Introduction.* Epworth
Press, 1938. 5s.
A thoroughly good, brief account of origins and relationships.

THOMPSON, J. M. *The Synoptic Gospels Arranged in Parallel
Columns.* Clarendon Press, 1910. 12s. 6d.
The best synopsis in English, showing the relationship between Mark, Luke and
Matthew: essential for a thorough understanding of the Gospels.

(d) THE LIFE AND TEACHING OF JESUS

*DEANE, ANTHONY. *The World Christ Knew.* Guild Books, 1946.
1s.
An excellent short sketch.

DODD, C. H. *Parables of the Kingdom.* Nisbet, 1935. 8s. 6d.

*GLOVER, T. R. *The Jesus of History.* S.C.M. Press, 1917. 2s. 6d.
Brings out from the Parables and the narrative portions of the Gospels, the
circumstances in which Jesus lived and taught, and the material that he used in
teaching.

GORE, CHARLES. *Jesus of Nazareth.* Home University Library,
1929. 3s. 6d.
A good short life of Christ; somewhat conservative.

MANSON, T. W. *The Teaching of Jesus.* Cambridge University
Press, 1945. 18s.
Advanced, but most valuable to the teacher in its description of the methods
of teaching which Jesus used and the content of His message.

MARTIN, HUGH. *The Parables of the Gospels and Their Meaning for
To-day.* S.C.M. Press, 1937. 7s. 6d.
Makes full use of modern scholarship in interpreting the parables: pre-eminently
a book for teachers.

MATHEWS, BASIL. *A Life of Jesus.* Oxford University Press, 1934.
8s. 6d.
Written with imagination but with close adherence to the data in the Gospels.

* Indicates books of the simpler kind.

*MATHEWS, BASIL. *A Little Life of Jesus.* (Illustrated.) Oxford
University Press, 1933. 6s.

Not a condensation of the foregoing, but briefer, and with more of the text of
the Gospels incorporated.

MATHEWS, BASIL. *The World in Which Jesus Lived.* (Illustrated.)
Oxford University Press, 1937. 6s.

An excellent sketch of political, social and religious conditions in the times of
Jesus and Paul.

MUIRHEAD, L. A. *The Times of Christ.* T. and T. Clark, 1907.
3s. 6d.

QUICK, O. C. *The Realism of Christ's Parables.* S.C.M. Press,
1931. 2s.

RAVEN, C. E. and RAVEN, E. *The Life and Teaching of Jesus Christ.*
Cambridge University Press, 1940. 4s.

Background and explanatory material gathered together in introductory
chapters; text so printed as to show successively Mark, Q, the special material
used by Luke and Matthew respectively, and those sections of the Fourth Gospel
which add to our historical information.

*ROWLEY, H. H. *An Outline of the Teaching of Jesus.* Lutterworth
Press, 1945. 1s. 6d.

An admirable short outline.

SCOTT, E. F. *The Ethical Teaching of Jesus.* Macmillan, 1924.
7s. 6d.

An excellent summary.

*SKINNER, CONRAD. *The Gospel of the Lord Jesus.* Hodder and
Stoughton, 1937. 5s.

Jesus and His teaching as a practising teacher presents them; contains a valuable
introduction on the teaching of Scripture.

(e) THE APOSTOLIC PERIOD

DEANE, A. C. *St Paul and his Letters.* Hodder and Stoughton,
1942. 7s. 6d.

A good sketch of the man and an interpretive paraphrase of all his letters.

DEISSMAN, G. A. *Paul: a study in social religious history* (translated
by W. E. WILSON). Hodder and Stoughton, 1926. 21s.

A valuable book for the teachers' library.

* Indicates books of the simpler kind.

DODD, C. H. *The Apostolic Preaching and its Developments.* Hodder and Stoughton, 1936. 5s.

Shows very clearly the essential unity between the interpretation of Christianity which appears in the Acts, the Pauline Epistles and the Johannine writings and the presentation of Jesus in the Gospels: important and illuminating for teachers.

DODD, C. H. *History and the Gospel.* Nisbet, 1938. 7s. 6d.

In many respects a sequel to the foregoing: brings out the reliability of the Gospels and the way in which the apostolic preaching and writings were controlled by the 'events plus meaning' recorded in the Gospels.

*FINDLAY, J. A. *The Acts of the Apostles.* S.C.M. Press, 1934. 6s.

A stimulating account of the beginnings of Christianity following the story in the Acts.

GLOVER, T. R. *Paul of Tarsus.* S.C.M. Press, 1925. 3s. 6d.

A vigorous interpretation, making great use of knowledge concerning conditions in the Roman Empire at the time.

*MATHEWS, BASIL. *Paul the Dauntless.* Black, 1918 (and reprinting). 7s. 6d.

A vivid story, utilising background material very carefully gathered during repeated visits to the scenes of the apostle's missionary work.

NOCK, A. D. *St Paul.* Home University Library, 1938. 3s. 6d.

A short but scholarly account.

SCOTT, C. A. ANDERSON. *St Paul the Man and Teacher.* Cambridge University Press, 1936. 5s.

An excellent biographical introduction and summary of teaching by excerpts from the Epistles in chronological order.

SCOTT, E. F. *Paul's Epistle to the Romans.* S.C.M. Press, 1947. 6s.

Treats the Epistle to the Romans as 'essentially a modern book' with a message for our world to-day.

LATER CHURCH HISTORY

BARKER, FRANCIS. *The Church of the Apostles and the Fathers.* S.P.C.K. 2s. 6d.

An account of the first thousand years of Christianity, with special attention to the growth of organisation and the formulation of belief.

BETTENSON, H. *Documents of the Christian Church.* Worlds Classics. Oxford University Press, 1943. 4s.

A cheap 'source-book', giving original documents; valuable in teaching.

BEVAN, EDWYN. *Christianity.* Home University Library, 1932. 5s.

A survey of Christian history to the present.

* Indicates books of the simpler kind.

*CARRICK SMITH, K. L. *The Church and the churches.* S.C.M. Press, 1948. 7s. 6d.

An up-to-date study of the beliefs of the leading Christian denominations, including the Roman Catholic.

CROSSE, G. *A Short History of the English Church.* Mowbray, 1947. 3s. 6d.

A popular short account of the Church of England.

*DIAMOND, LUCY. *How the Gospel Came to Britain.* (Illustrated.) Oxford University Press. 6s.

A record beginning before the Roman occupation and continuing to the death of Bede; suitable for 14-year-old children.

DUNCAN-JONES, C. M. (ed.). *An Outline of Church History, from the Acts of the Apostles to the Reformation.* Allen and Unwin, 4 Parts, 1938, 1939. 4s. 6d. per volume.

Broadcasts by eminent scholars to the upper forms of schools.

FOSTER, J. *Then and Now.* S.C.M. Press, 1942. 6s.

FOSTER, J. *The World Church.* S.C.M. Press, 1945. 6s.

Two books on Church History which take into account the history of Christianity in the Far East.

GLOVER, T. R. *The Conflict of Religions in the Early Roman Empire.* Methuen, 1932. 11s. 6d.

A classic book dealing with the period.

LATOURETTE, K. S. *The Unquenchable Light.* Eyre and Spottiswoode, 1945. 7s. 6d.

A condensation of the author's classic 7-volume work on 'The Expansion of Christianity'.

McNEILE, R. F. *Christianity in Southern Fenland.* Bowes and Bowes, 1948. 12s. 6d.

Contains a wealth of information about the local history of Christianity in Cambridgeshire.

MACY, S. B. *The Army of God.* S.P.C.K. Reprinting. 2s. 6d.

Simple and graphic: church history down to the time of Gregory and Augustine of Canterbury.

MILFORD, C. S. *South India's New Church.* Edinburgh House Press, 1947. 6d.

PAYNE, E. A. *The Free Church Tradition in England.* S.C.M. Press, 1944. 6s.

* Indicates books of the simpler kind.

*SOMERVELL, D. C. *A Short History of Our Religion.* Bell, 1925. 6s.

Begins with the history contained in the Bible, and brings the story down through the ages to the present day.

*STEPHEN, DOROTHEA. *Outline History of the Christian Church.* S.P.C.K. Reprinting. 2s. 6d.

Concise but comprehensive; contains a chapter on each of the great Christian communions.

WALKER, VERA. *A First Church History.* S.C.M. Press, 1936. 7s. 6d.

A clear and well-balanced outline, with time-chart, from the early Church to modern times.

A Christian Year Book. S.C.M. Press, 1947. 5s.

The Ecumenical Movement. (Discussion Group Pamphlets No. 14.) S.P.C.K., 1947. 1s.

CHRISTIAN BELIEF AND CONDUCT

Archbishops' Commission. *Doctrine in the Church of England.* S.P.C.K., 1938. 4s.

BAILLIE, D. M. *God was in Christ.* Faber, 1948. 16s.

BALMFORTH, H. *The Christian Religion.* S.P.C.K., 1945. 4s.

BLUNT, A. W. F. *The Faith of the Catholic Church.* Oxford University Press, 1940. 5s.

The origin, development and significance of the Creeds.

FENN, J. E. (ed.). *How Christians Worship.* S.C.M. Press, 1942. 2s. 6d.

GREENWOOD, W. O. *Biology and Christian Belief.* S.C.M. Press, 1938. 5s.

A competent statement of facts and a lucid discussion of issues well adapted to the use of both teachers and sixth form pupils.

HUNKIN, J. W. *Is it Reasonable to Believe?* Hodder and Stoughton, 1935. 3s.

An interpretation of the Apostles' Creed and straightforward discussion of the relationship between its affirmations and modern thought, especially scientific.

LINDSAY, A. D. *The Two Moralities.* Eyre and Spottiswoode, 1940. 6s.

Deals with the conflict of loyalties in the modern state.

* Indicates books of the simpler kind.

LINDSAY, A. D. *The Moral Teaching of Jesus.* Hodder and Stoughton, 1937. 2s. 6d.

*LUMB, J. R. *Power and Witness.* S.P.C.K., 1938. 2s. 6d.
Thirty-seven lessons for young people.

MATTHEWS, W. R. *The Christian Faith.* Essays in Explanation and Defence. Eyre and Spottiswoode, 1936. 10s. 6d.
By Anglican and Free Church scholars and teachers, on 'subjects fundamental in Christian Belief', such as the Inspiration and Authority of the Bible, Christian Belief in God, the Historical Value of the Gospels, the Primitive Church, Sin and Redemption, the Church, Christian Worship, the Christian Way of Life: of very great value to teachers.

RAVEN, C. E. *Science, Religion and the Future.* Cambridge University Press, 1943. 7s. 6d.
Popular lectures given to a general audience in Cambridge.

*REID, JAMES. *Why Be Good?* Hodder and Stoughton, Westminster Books, 1935. 3s. 6d.
An excellent discussion of moral and social practice leading back to religious principle.

RICHARDSON, ALAN. *Christian Apologetics.* S.C.M. Press, 1947. 10s. 6d.

RIDDELL, J. G. *What We Believe.* Church of Scotland Publications Committee. 5s.
Explanations for young people of the Church, Creeds and Sacraments as these are interpreted by the Presbyterian Church and in general by most of the Free Churches.

RITCHIE, A. D. *Civilisation, Science and Religion.* Pelican, 1945. 1s. 6d.
A study of scientific methods and concepts and the place of the life of the spirit in the modern world.

SAYERS, DOROTHY. *The Mind of the Maker.* Methuen, 1948. 6s.

*SKINNER, CONRAD. *Approach to Church Membership.* Epworth Press, 1946. 5s.
A simple discussion of the implications of Church membership.

TEMPLE, WILLIAM. *Christianity and the Social Order.* Penguin Special, 1942. 1s. 6d.
A brief justification of the Church's concern for social questions.

* Indicates books of the simpler kind.

God's Will for Church and Nation. Reports by Church of Scotland Committees on Social Questions. 1946. 7s. 6d.

TYRRELL, G. N. M. *The Personality of Man*. Pelican, 1947. 1s. 6d.

A scientific study of the data of psychic phenomena. Gives the results of the most recent psychical research in non-technical language by the President of the Society for Psychical Research.

WALTON, R. *What do Christians Really Believe?* S.C.M. Press, 1944. 1s.

A brief statement of the Faith written for senior pupils with questions for discussion and a short bibliography.

WHALE, J. S. *Christian Doctrine*. Cambridge University Press, 1942. 7s. 6d.

A concise account of the leading doctrines of the Faith written in popular language.

WILLIAMS, J. G. *God—and His World*. A book about Worship. S.P.C.K. Reprinting. 5s.

Lessons for the Sundays throughout a year dealing with Matter and Spirit, Human Society and Divine.

WRIGHT, R. S. *Asking Them Questions*. Oxford University Press, 1938. 2 vols. 4s. 6d. each.

Brief answers by representative theologians and teachers to difficult questions about religion and life asked by older boys and girls.

Note. In a footnote to the Note on 'Miracles' on p. 151 five books are referred to which are not mentioned in this list, and others not included will be found at the end of the section 'Specific Books as Separate Courses' for sixth forms on p. 133.

COMPARATIVE RELIGION

BALLOU, R. O. *The Bible of the World*. Kegan Paul, 1940. 18s.

Contains selections from the Scriptures of the great religions of the world.

*BOUQUET, A. C. *Comparative Religion: a short outline*. Pelican, 1941. 1s.

A simple and straightforward treatment of the subject.

KELLETT, E. E. *A Short History of Religions*. Gollancz, 1933. 5s.

PATON, W. *Jesus Christ and the World's Religions*. Edinburgh House Press, 1927. 1s.

* Indicates books of the simpler kind.

THEORY AND PRACTICE

(a) STORY METHOD AND BIOGRAPHICAL MATERIAL

GARLICK, PHYLLIS L. *Pioneers of the Kingdom.* Highway Press, 1946. Complete 7s. 6d., or Parts I, II or III, 3s. each.

Stories of men and women noteworthy in the expansion of Christianity from the First Century till now.

GILL, D. M. and PULLEN, A. M. *Adventures of Service.* S.C.M. Press, 1938. 2s. 6d.

Collections of stories from the lives of contemporary Christians who have wrought great things in many differing spheres of life.

GREGORY, SIR RICHARD. *Discovery, or the Spirit and Service of Science.* Phillips, 1916. 5s.

Contains stories of the pioneers of science, useful to illustrate the spirit of service.

HAYES, E. H. *Yarns on Social Pioneers.* Religious Education Press, 1930. 1s. 6d.

A series of biographical sketches—John Wyclif, Elizabeth Fry and six others. There are seven other titles in the series, 1928-34.

MATHEWS, BASIL. *The Adventures of Paul.* (Illustrated.) Oxford University Press, 1945. 6s.

A popular account written for ages 12-16.

SANDS, P. C. *Modern Illustrations of the Gospels.* S.P.C.K., 1938. 2s. 6d.

Incidents from the lives of saints, missionaries and reformers, used to light up the teaching of the Gospels.

SAYERS, D. *The Man Born to be King.* Gollancz. (Cheap Edition 1947.) 6s.

A series of vivid plays on the life of Christ, originally written for broadcasting.

The Adult School Study Handbook. Annual. National Adult School Union. 2s. 6d. and 3s. 6d.

Contains a great deal of biographical material useful for the teacher.

The Teacher's Bookshelf. Religious Education Press. Gratis.

Contains many biographical collections as well as particulars of Teachers' Guides to the Agreed Syllabuses, which provide material for the teacher, and one of which, *Christianity Goes Into Action*, 1946, contains a number of biographical sketches.

(b) For the Youngest Children (under 7)

The Little Children's Bible. Cambridge University Press, 1947. 1s. 6d.

Barnard, W. E. and Spriggs, E. H. *Tales to Tell, More Tales to Tell.* Religious Education Press, 1942, 1943. 3s. 6d.

Chalmers, M. J. *Bible Stories for children from 4–6 years.* Nelson, 1933. 2s. 6d.

Chalmers, M. J. and Entwistle, M. *Bible Books for Small People.* S.C.M. Press, 1933. 2s. 6d.

Cox, L. E. *God's Friendly People.* Religious Education Press, 1939. 1s. 6d.

Nicholl, Noel E. *Before Jesus Came.* Lutterworth Press, 1934. 4s. 6d.
Old Testament stories for little children.

Thomas, J. Gale. *Our Father.* Mowbray, 1940. 2s. 6d.
The Lord's Prayer in pictures and verses.

(c) For Young Children (aged 7–11)

The Children's Bible. Cambridge University Press, 1947. 2s. 9d.

Cooper, I. Shewell. *Foundations of the Kingdom.* S.P.C.K. 2s. 6d.
Lessons on the Old Testament for Juniors.

Cosgrave, Joyce. *The Story of Amos the Prophet* and other titles. S.P.C.K. 8d. each.

Gurney, E. B. *Children of the Wilderness.* Oxford University Press. 7s. 6d.
Shows how use may be made of archaeological discovery.

Krall, B. C. *Stories of Favourite Saints.* Religious Education Press, 1943. 3s. 6d.

Krall, B. C. *Stories Jesus Heard, Other Stories Jesus Heard.* Religious Education Press, 1947. 3s. 6d.

Nicholl, Noel E. *The Children's Jesus.* Lutterworth Press, 1932. 4s. 6d.

WHITE, H. COSTLEY *St Luke's Story of Jesus.* S.P.C.K., 1943. 5s.

WHITE, H. COSTLEY and HARWOOD, J. *Bible Picture Books.* S.C.M. Press. 1s. each.

(d) AIMS AND METHODS

AVERY, M. *Lesson Notes on the Old Testament.* National Society and S.P.C.K., 1941. 3s.

Board of Education Consultative Committee on *Secondary Education* (*The Spens Report,* H.M. Stationery Office, 3s. 6d.), reprint of *Chapter V,* 'Scripture'. Institute of Christian Education. 6d.
Of first importance as a statement of principles and an indication of methods.

BRALEY, E. F. *The Teaching of Religion.* Longmans, 1938. 3s. 6d.
A practical handbook.

CLARK, M. E. A. *Methods of Teaching Religion to Children.* S.P.C.K., 1946. 5s.

COLLINS, FREDA. *Children in the Market Place.* University of London Press, 1942. 6s. 6d.
Principles of religious drama, practical suggestions and bibliography.

DENT, PHYLLIS M. *Teaching Doctrine.* National Society. 1s. 3d.

HEAWOOD, GEOFFREY L. *Religion in School.* S.C.M. Press, 1939. 7s. 6d.
A valuable discussion of religion in a secondary school.

LUMB, J. R. *Religious Instruction in Elementary Schools.* S.P.C.K., 1939. 3s. 6d.
A manual for teachers.

MUMFORD, E. READ. *Understanding our Children.* Longmans, 1937. 5s. 6d.
Formerly published under the title 'The Dawn of Character'; deals with younger children.

MURRAY, A. V. *The School and the Church.* S.C.M. Press, 1945. 3s. 6d.
Discusses the theological implications of religious education

NEWBY, CATHARINE R. *An Introduction to Child Study for Teachers of Religion.* National Society, 1945. 4s. 6d.

REEVES, MARJORIE. *Growing up in a Modern Society.* University of London Press, 1946. 4s. 6d.
Puts Christian education in the setting of modern society.

RICHARDS, G. A. *The Teaching of Christian Doctrine.* Religious Education Press, 1946. 5s.
Discusses individual doctrines and gives useful notes.

SANDHURST, B. G. *How Heathen is Britain?* Collins, 1946. 3s. 6d.
Contains an illuminating survey of the teaching of Scripture in Britain.

WHANSLAW, H. M. *Making Bible Models.* Religious Education Press, 1945. 2s.

WILSON, DOROTHY F. *Child Psychology and Religious Education.* S.C.M. Press, 1928. 2s. 6d.
Particularly good in relation to younger children.

YEAXLEE, B. A. *Religion and the Growing Mind.* Nisbet, 1939. 7s. 6d.
Discusses the religious development of children and adolescents in the light of modern psychology, with chapters for parents and teachers.

The Religious Education of Children under the Age of Seven Years, Considered from the standpoint of Modern Psychology. The Religious Education of Children between Seven and Eleven Years. The Religious Education of Pupils between Eleven to Sixteen Years of Age. Institute of Christian Education. 1s. each.
Each by a group of practising teachers, ministers and psychologists.

The following, written primarily for Sunday School teachers, are the outcome of wide experience in other forms of education also and will be found thoroughly practical:

GILL, D. M. and PULLEN, A. M. *Methods of Teaching for Sunday Schools To-day.* National Sunday School Union, 1936. 2s. 6d.
Contains suggestions for dramatisation, projects and other practical methods.

RUSSELL, B. *Leading the Children.* S.P.C.K., 1947. 3s.

WORSHIP

(a) SERVICE BOOKS

The Daily Service: Prayers and Hymns for Schools. Oxford University Press. 1939. 1s. 3d. (Full music edition, 6s.)

Contains two or three full forms of service for each morning of the week. Each day is devoted to a different theme, which thus gives a complete unity to each act of worship. The Daily Prayers are bound up with over 200 hymns and carols admirably chosen and arranged, under the musical editorship of Drs Vaughan Williams and Martin Shaw.

The Oxford Book of School Worship. S.P.C.K. 1935. Part I: Infants, 1s. 6d. Parts II and III: Juniors and Seniors, 3s. 6d.

Though prepared for Church of England Schools, no teacher would find the series difficult to adapt or could fail to derive suggestions and help from them. Parts II and III might be difficult to use unless in the hands of the pupils.

A Service Book for Youth. Ed. Dr S. M. E. TROOD. S.P.C.K. 1938. 1s. 6d.

Over 80 well-ordered short services, each containing verse, readings, responsory, short litany, Lord's Prayer and endings, and dealing with a single theme, usually a Christian virtue, but providing also for the seasons of the Christian year and other special occasions.

The School Service. Ed. DORIS SMITH. Religious Education Press. 1945. 6s.

(b) SCRIPTURE READINGS

The Little Children's Bible. Cambridge University Press. 1947. 1s. 6d.

The Children's Bible. Cambridge University Press. 1947. 2s. 9d.

The Cambridge Senior Bible. Ed. K. M. RICHES. Cambridge University Press. 1945. 3s. 6d.

The Little Bible. Oxford University Press. 1931. 3s. 9d.

Contains a scheme of readings arranged as a companion to *Prayers and Hymns for Schools.*

A Short Bible in the Authorised Version. Blackwell. 1946. 4s. 3d.

The Daily Reading. Oxford University Press. 1939. 4s. 6d.

Designed as a companion to the Daily Service (which itself has references to passages arranged under subject-headings), and arranged according to the same general theme: suited to all forms and ages.

Two minute Bible Readings. S.C.M. Press. 1945. 5s.

A useful selection.

(c) PRAYERS

Collections of Prayers are bewilderingly numerous. Only a few of the best and most comprehensive are mentioned below.

An Anthology of Prayers. Ed. A. S. T. FISHER. Longmans. 1934. 4s. 6d.

A good selection, admirably indexed.

A Book of Prayers for Schools. S.C.M. Press. 1936. 7s. 6d.

A Book of Prayers for Students. S.C.M. Press. 1921.

A Chain of Prayer across the Ages. Ed. SELINA FOX. Murray. 1930. 5s.

These are large and comprehensive collections containing prayers of all ages and accents, but of varying merit.

JAMES, LIONEL, *Jubilate Deo.* Oxford University Press. 1940. 2s.

A collection of prayers classified in a way very useful for schools, with suggestions as to its use.

Daily Prayer. Ed. G. W. BRIGGS and E. MILNER-WHITE. Oxford University Press. 1941. 5s. 6d.

A collection prepared for use with *The Daily Service* and *The Daily Reading*.

FERGUSON, J. M. *Look Upon a Little Child.* Religious Education Press. 1945. 2s. 6d.

GARLICK, P. L. *All our Friends.* Highway Press. 1938. 4s. 6d. and 6d.

SIMPSON, N. and COX, L. E. *Children's Praises.* S.C.M. Press. 1934.

TEMPEST, MARGARET. *A Thanksgiving for Children.* Collins. 1944. 2s. 6d.

THOMAS, J. GALE. *Our Father*. Mowbray. 1940.

WILSON, A. *My Thank You Book*. Carey Press. 1946. 2*s*. 6*d*. and
1*s*. 6*d*.
The foregoing are intended for young children.

(*d*) HYMNS AND MUSIC

The Daily Service: Prayers and Hymns for Schools. Revised Edition.
1947. Oxford University Press. 7*s*. 6*d*.
Contains over 200 hymns and carols, as noted above.

Prayers and Hymns for use in Schools. Oxford University Press.
1928. 2*s*. 9*d*. and 3*s*. 3*d*.

Prayers and Hymns for Junior Schools. Oxford University Press.
1933. 2*s*. 6*d*.

Prayers and Hymns for Little Children. Oxford University Press.
1932. 1*s*. 8*d*.
The foregoing are under the musical editorship of Drs VAUGHAN WILLIAMS and
MARTIN SHAW.

Hymns of the Kingdom. Oxford University Press. 1923. 6*s*.
Contains 200 hymns; edited by SIR WALFORD DAVIES.

The Oxford Book of Carols. Oxford University Press. Music
Edition, 8*s*. 6*d*., words (limp cloth), 1*s*. 9*d*.

The Church and School Hymnal. S.P.C.K.

CROPPER, MARGARET and WYLOM, A. R. B. *Hymns and Songs for
the Church Kindergarten*. S.P.C.K. 1939. 4*s*.

DAVIES, SIR WALFORD and GRACE, HARVEY. *Music and Worship*.
Eyre and Spottiswoode. 1935. 6*s*.

WISEMAN, H. *Children Praising*. Oxford University Press. 1937.
5*s*.
Words edited by W. H. Hamilton.

(e) GENERAL

The Inner Light. Allen and Unwin. Two volumes. 1936. 5s.

An anthology of Scripture sentences and memorable sayings by Christian writers in all centuries. The latter should often be helpful in emphasising the significance of the daily service in fresh and living ways. The whole is arranged under a wide variety of themes.

ABBOTT, ERIC. *Escape or Freedom.* Heffer. 1939. 2s. 6d.

CLEMENTS, BERNARD. *When Ye Pray.* S.C.M. Press. 1940. 1s.

CLEMENTS, BERNARD. *How to Pray.* S.P.C.K. 1930. 2d.

FOSDICK, H. E. *The Meaning of Prayer.* S.C.M. Press. 1916. 4s. 6d.

Contains many short passages of Scripture and notable prayers, set in an admirably helpful survey of the subject of prayer. The same author's *The Meaning of Faith* and *The Meaning of Service* may also be found useful.

GORE, C. *Prayer and the Lord's Prayer.* Allen and Unwin. 1946. 2s. 6d.

LUMB, R. *The Groundwork of Prayer.* Faith Press. 1942. 5s. 6d.

PECK, DAVID. *Living Worship.* 1944. Eyre and Spottiswoode. 4s. 6d.

UNDERHILL, EVELYN. *Worship.* Nisbet. 1936. 10s. 6d.

WYON, OLIVE. *School of Prayer.* S.C.M. Press. 1943. 6s.

APPENDIX

THE CONFERENCE

The members of the Conference appointed to draw up the Syllabus were:

Representing the Authority

Dr T. S. HELE, Master of Emmanuel College (Chairman).

The Rev. J. BURNABY, Fellow and Dean of Chapel of Trinity College.

The Rev. C. H. DODD, D.D., Norris-Hulse Professor of Divinity and Fellow of Jesus College.

Mr WALTER OAKESHOTT, Headmaster of Winchester College.

Dr R. H. THOULESS, Fellow of Corpus Christi College.

Dr W. G. HUMPHREY, Headmaster of The Leys School.

The Rev. C. F. D. MOULE, Fellow of Clare College.

Miss E. M. VERINI, Principal of the Cambridge Training College for Women.

Mr M. C. BURKITT, County Councillor, University Lecturer in Prehistoric Archaeology.

Mr E. G. G. FROST, County Alderman.

Representing the Church of England

The Rev. S. F. ALLISON, Principal of Ridley Hall.

The Rev. Canon H. BALMFORTH, Principal of Ely Theological College.

The Rev. H. M. J. BANTING.

The Rev. W. O. CHADWICK, Fellow of Trinity Hall.

Miss M. E. HUDSON, Principal of Hockerill Training College.

The Rev. J. R. LUMB.

The Rev. A. WAYMENT, Director of Religious Education, Diocese of Ely.

The Rev. Canon A. L. WOODARD, Adviser in Schools, Church of England Council for Education.

Representing the Cambridge and District Free Church Federal Council

The Rev. E. C. BLACKMAN, Tutor of Cheshunt College.

Miss ANNE BRADFIELD, Homerton College.

The Rev. J. Y. CAMPBELL, D.D., Westminster College.

Mrs ELIZABETH DIAMOND.

Mr A. VICTOR MURRAY, Principal of Cheshunt College.

The Rev. W. VELLAM PITTS, Secretary, Cambridge Free Church Federal Council.

The Rev. J. N. Schofield, University Lecturer in Hebrew and Old Testament Subjects.

The Rev. Conrad Skinner, Chaplain of The Leys School.

Representing the Teachers

Mr E. Armitage, Headmaster of Soham Grammar School.

Mr A. Beckley, Central Boys' School, Cambridge.

Mr T. H. Bray, Headmaster of Cherryhinton School.

Miss M. H. Cattley, formerly Headmistress of the Perse Girls' School.

Mrs I. S. Farrow, Cambridgeshire High School for Girls.

Mr E. Foster, Second Master, Sawston Village College.

Mr W. E. Gumbrell, Cambridgeshire High School for Boys.

Miss B. C. Hinkins, Milton Road School, Cambridge.

Mr P. W. Lovering, Headmaster of Soham Boys' County School.

Mr F. J. Mansfield, Central Boys' School, Cambridge.

Miss A. M. Musther, Headmistress of Bottisham Junior County School.

Mr A. J. Parr, Warden of Impington Village College.

Miss H. A. Strathdee, Headmistress of Histon Junior County School.

Miss S. L. Thompson, Headmistress of St George's Girls' School, Cambridge.

Secretary
Mr Henry Morris, C.B.E.

Chairman of the Drafting Committee
The Rev. J. Burnaby.

Secretary to the Drafting Committee
Mr Thurstan Shaw.

The following assisted the Drafting Sub-Committees as co-opted members:

Miss A. M. Battensby, Headmistress of the Cambridgeshire High School for Girls.

Mrs M. C. Burkitt.

Miss K. M. Howlett, Morley Memorial Infants' School.

Mr B. Newton John, Headmaster of the Cambridgeshire High School for Boys.

Miss M. A. Scott, Headmistress of the Perse Girls' School.

Mr S. Stubbs, Headmaster of the Perse Boys' School.

Memoranda were received from the Rev. Canon Spencer Leeson and the Rev. Basil Yeaxlee, and the Institute of Christian Education gave help in the preparation of the list of books for reference.